COSMIC RELIGION

Cosmic Religion

by

JUNG YOUNG LEE

PHILOSOPHICAL LIBRARY
NEW YORK, N. Y.

Copyright, © 1973, by Philosophical Library, Inc.
15 East 40th Street, New York, N. Y. 10016

Library of Congress Catalog Card No. 73-82163
SBN 8022-2125-4

Manufactured in the United States of America

Dedicated to

MY WIFE *and* MY CHILDREN

Who taught me the cosmic significance
of my existence

CONTENTS

Introduction

The root of our ecological and existential problems is primarily due to the misrepresentation of our religious thinking in the West. It is the religious orientation which has shaped the attitude of Western people toward nature and God. Nature has become the counterpart of divine activity and the enemy of human perfection. A natural man is damned as a heathen, and an unnatural man is elevated as a civilized Christian. Man's domination over nature is encouraged as his virtue, and his retreat to nature is discouraged as a sign of disgrace. Thus the conflict between man and nature becomes inevitable. The separation of man from nature is eventually the separation from himself, for he is a part of nature. This separation of oneself, which creates the inner conflict, is the very root of his existential problems. Thus, our ecological and existential problems are inseparable. They are mutually interdependent. In order to deal with these problems, the religious orientation which has caused them must be reassessed.

The failure of traditional religion in the West is mainly in the use of exclusive symbols for the inclusive God. The symbols of God such as the King, Lord, Master, Saviour, etc. are personal names. By attributing personal names or symbols to God, the non-personal existence is almost completely neglected from the sphere of our religious thinking.

The God who is excluded from the non-personal existence cannot be the Creator and Preserver of all things. Thus, God must transcend a personal category. God is the God of both personal and non-personal (or impersonal) existence. Therefore, the traditional religious thinking which has eliminated the concerns of non-personal existence from the religious framework is a tragic failure in the West.

Cosmic religion transcends both personal and non-personal categories. It presupposes the God of all things, who is the cosmic God. This God is the God of man, the God of tree, the God of stone, the God of water, the God of air, and the God of everything that exists. The cosmic God is a personal God to persons and a non-personal God to non-persons. The cosmic God is "He" to men but "It" to stones and trees. This kind of God transcends religions, creeds, nationalities, races, species, forms, qualities, space and time. Thus, cosmic religion which deals with the cosmic God, the God of the whole and *for* the whole, is essentially universal religion.

What, then, is the meaningful symbol of the cosmic God? Since the cosmic God transcends a personal category, we must find the symbol of God prior to personal symbols being attributed to him. The most primordial symbol of God in the Judeo-Christian faith is found in Exodus 3:14, where God is known as "I am what I am" or "I become what I become." "This is," as Suzuki said, "a most profound utterance, for all our religious or spiritual or metaphysical experiences start from it." [1] The cosmic God is, then, the subject or the source of "becoming." The cosmos is constantly in the process of becoming, because change is the essential characteristic of cosmic process. In other words, what makes becoming possible is the Change which changes all things. Thus, it is said, "The Change is the begetter of all begetting." [2] The Change which changes

---

[1] D. T. Suzuki, *Mysticism: Christian and Buddhist* (N. Y.: Harper and Row, 1957), pp. 76, 77.

[2] *Ta Chuan*, Sec. I, Ch. 5.

all into the process of becoming is *Tao*,[3] the ultimate reality, which transcends both being and becoming as well as personal and non-personal categories at the same time. The essence of cosmos is not the unchanging being but the changing becoming, because change is the essence of every becoming. Cosmic religion is, then, based on the idea that everything changes into the process of becoming because of the cosmic God who is change itself. Therefore, cosmic religion is none other than changeology, for it is a religion of change.

This is not written to undercut the profundity of Christian or any other religious teaching. Rather, it is hoped for the vivification of that profundity viable to the growing interest in the cosmic process of man's becoming. I do not intend this to be the complete and comprehensive treatise on cosmic religion. Rather, it is only an initial move toward the process which may eventually focus our attention on the cosmic significance of religious truth. Therefore, this is written for those who are open to new possibilities in the search for truth. If this small volume can provide seeds of thought for a fresh and creative approach of religion to the wholeness of man and cosmos, it has achieved its purpose.

---

[3] *"Tao* is . . . in one word change itself." See Ch'u Chai and Winberg Chai, ed., *I Ching: Book of Changes,* tr. by James Legge (New Hyde Park: University Books, 1964), pp. xl-xli. See also Jung Young Lee, *Principle of Changes: Understanding the I Ching* (New Hyde Park: University Books. 1971), pp. 74-86.

COSMIC RELIGION

I. The Change

The Change is the beginning and the end of all process. Everything is in a process of becoming because of the Change. The Change is in everything, but everything is not the Change. The Change is both hidden in the depth of all things and manifest in the concrete process of becoming. The Change is not known by itself but by its manifestation only. It is manifest in everything, because everything owes its existence to the Change.

Day changes to night and night to day because of the Change. Brightness changes to darkness and dark to bright because of the Change. Spring changes to summer and summer to autumn because of the Change. Coldness becomes warmth and warmth becomes coldness because of the Change. The Change makes trees grow and decay. Man is born and dies because he is part of the Change. The way of our thinking changes, the manner of our behavior changes, the system of our values changes, for the Change is active in all things. The strong becomes weak and the weak becomes strong because of the Change. The future becomes the present and the present becomes the past because of the Change. The Change makes the small great and the great small. Energy changes to mass and mass to energy, for they are relative to the power of the Change. Everything is in the process of change because of the Change. In the process of becoming changing can be gradual or rapid, for everything has its own trend in the changing process. The process of change is total and universal, for the Change is the inner essence of all existence.

The Change is the mother of everything that exists in the universe. Being is possible because of becoming, and becoming is possible because of the Change. Being is not real by itself, but is real only in the process of becoming. Being itself is nothing but the illusion of becoming. Being is our misunderstanding of becoming. Being is our mental particularization of becoming, while becoming is the wholeness of being realized in the process of change. It is not the being which makes becoming possible, but the becoming which makes being real. Being is totally dependent on becoming, for it is always relative to the Change. Becoming is not dependent on being but is meaningful because of being. Becoming is the realization of the Change, while being is the realization of becoming. Thus, without the Change becoming is not possible, and without becoming being is an illusion. The Change is the source of all creative process, because it has creativity within itself. The process of creativity through production and reproduction is possible because of the Change. Whenever there is growth and decay or expansion and contraction, there must be the Change. The Change is the moving mover of all the changes in the process of becoming.

The Change is the inner essence of all becomings. It is the subtlest of all subtleties and the deepest abyss of all grounds. It is the all-embracing, all-penetrating, and all-fulfilling reality. It is absurd to our mind, but its manifestation is concrete. It is manifest in both personal and impersonal categories of becoming. The Change itself is neither personal nor impersonal in nature. It is both personal and impersonal reality at the same time. It transcends all the categorical distinctions of human expression. It is beyond our knowing and comprehending. It is not the Change if it is known to us. The Change that is known is not the real Change. It is too deep to comprehend and too subtle to express in human words. It is so pure that no discrimination is possible. The Change itself does not have any form or category. Any form of discrimination and differentiation is born in the process of becoming. Thus the Change is known only in its concrete manifestation. The Change itself is the Void, the negation of all discrimination and differentiation. It is the extinction of all dichotomy and separation. Everything has its origin in this Void, which is none other than a pure potentiality. The manifestation of the Change is impermanent and transitory, but the Change itself is eternal. Everything changes because of the Change, but the Change itself is changeless. All things are relative to the Change, but the Change alone is absolute.

The Change itself is absolute but its manifestation is relative. They are not two separate things. The Change that is absolute is also the Change that is relative. The former is the Change itself, and the latter is the realization of the Change in the world. The Change is represented by a symbol of zero, which is neither positive nor negative. It is the origin of differentiations between the positive and the negative and between expansion and contraction. In it all positive and negative as well as expanding and contracting numbers are inherent, but the total sum of numbers cannot approximate it. Thus zero is the symbol of Void, which is total negation and total affirmation of all things at the same time. The Change also takes a symbol of embryo, which contains all possible becomings in the world but is more than a mere process of becoming. Rather all becomings are inherent in it. The Change is also analogous with the ever-swelling germ, where what is not relative and what is potentially relative are present at the same time. It is both the changing Change and the changeless Change simultaneously. It is changeless, yet changes all things. Changelessness and change are essentially inseparable in the Change. There is change because of changelessness and there is changelessness because of change. In the Change, changelessness and change are united and become the undifferentiated continuum. Because of this wholeness the

Change is also both transcendent and immanent at the same time. Thus the Change that is changeless is known as God, Logos, Tao, Brahman, and many other names. It is the essence of all cosmic energy and the background of all things in the universe.

The Change works through two hands. By the interplay of these two opposites the Change is manifest in all things. Since everything is of the Change, everything has two poles of interplay. The very process of becoming begins with this interplay. The differentiation and discrimination are born out of the undifferentiated continuum because of this interaction of opposites. These opposites are primary categories of all differentiated discontinuation. These counterparts are everywhere, because everything is in the process of becoming. Anything that changes has the interplay of the opposites. These two counterparts possess the archaic symbols of yin and yang. In physical science, yin is called a negative energy, and yang is called a positive energy. In the process of action, yin is known as the passive and yang is known as the active. In the description of space, yin is known as the rear and yang is known as the front. In the description of direction, yin is known as the west and yang as the east. In the category of dimension, yin is known as below and yang as above. In the description of character, yin is known as tenderness and yang as firmness. These two opposite hands or yin and yang are expressed in all things. Yin and yang are the bases of the sub-atomic structures, which are regarded as the microcosms of the universe. Therefore, everything can be reduced to these two poles of yin and yang. Things are different, because they are manifestations of the different combinations of yin and yang. Since yin and yang are the basic constituents of everything which changes, everything is of the Change.

The primacy of these two opposites is found in the story of creation. The differentiation of light from darkness was the beginning of creation. Light represents yang and darkness represents yin. The next was the differentiation of heaven from earth, and then that of water from the dry land. Heaven is the dimension of above and earth is that of below. Thus the former represents yang and the latter yin. Water represents yin and a dry land represents yang. Finally, the differentiation of man from woman marks the end of the story of creation. Man represents yang and woman represents yin. Therefore, the story of creation is the story of the interplay of two opposites. The differentiation of two opposites is the way of change. As long as the interplay of yin and yang takes place, the process of creation continues towards the process of re-creation. In the process of change there is no beginning and ending. Creation as this process will continue forever.

The Change is patient. It does not force the world into a uniform rate of change. It allows room for the differences of individual characters in the process of change. Some have the inclination to change fast, and others are apt to change slowly. The Change goes along with various dispositions of individual becoming. It never forces them to be other than true to themselves. Nevertheless, there is a definite trend of change in all things. When the sun reaches its zenith, it begins to decline. When the moon is full, it starts to wane. High mountains become valleys, and valleys become hills. Joy becomes sorrow, and happiness turns to tragedy. The last becomes the first, and modesty wins love. When one reaches its utmost, it must retreat. Everything that expands to a certain limit must revert to its opposite. Each has its own limitation. Within this limitation growth and decay or expansion and contraction take place. Nothing can grow or expand forever. One grows to a certain degree and then retreats again to decay. Trees do not grow forever. They grow to a certain height and then begin to decay. The universe cannot expand forever. It must contract again when it expands to its maximum. Yin cannot grow forever. When it is full, it starts to revert to its minimum. Yang cannot grow forever. When it is full, it also reverts to its opposite. When yin grows, yang decays. When yang grows, yin decays. They are mutually interdependent. Through the constant interplay of yin and yang in a reverse order, the certain trend of expansion and contraction or growth and decay is evident in all things.

The way of the Change is not conflict but the complementarity of opposites. None of them is sufficient by itself. The positive energy is not sufficient by itself. It needs the negative energy to fulfill its incompleteness. A male is not complete by himself. He needs his counterpart, a female, to complement his incompleteness. The sound is not sufficient by itself. It needs the silence as the background of its activity. One cannot experience joy without sorrow. The experience of suffering is known when love is experienced. When one is sufficient by itself, it does not require its counterpart. Self-sufficiency breaks down the delicate balance of counterpoles and produces conflict and disorder. That is not the proper way of the Change. Everything that changes is not sufficient by itself, but the Change alone is sufficient. When the Change is at work, all things are in complementarity to make the rounded whole. Light and darkness are not in conflict but complementary to each other. Light exists in its background, darkness. Darkness can exist because of its counterpart, light. Both of them are limited. When light reaches a certain peak, it begins to yield itself to darkness. When darkness reaches its utmost intensity, it begins to yield itself to light. Right and wrong are not in conflict, but complementary to each other. Right is possible because of wrong, and wrong is real because of right. Both right and wrong are relative to each other and mutually sustain each other. Nothing that is of the Change is absolute by itself. Everything necessitates its counterpart to complete its insufficiency. The insufficiency of one makes its counterpart necessary, so that harmony and unity in the Change are realized within a certain limit. The Change does not value one over the other. It does not exalt one over the other. It is also a peacemaker between the conflicting interests of yin and yang. It is the way of fulfilling mutual satisfactions to bring them in peace and harmony.

The Change is spontaneous. It is the inner tendency which

takes the natural course. It is natural because it is not motivated. The Change is like an infant child whose expressions are not constrained by compulsion. It moves like the unfolding leaves of flowers in the morning. It is free like the wind in the open air. Its movement is as subtle as the growth of trees. It is the inner movement which makes the natural development possible. The Change is both the active impulse of life and the passive response to death. It makes the inner process of growth possible. It moves all without moving. It changes all without changing. It procreates all without effort. It does not have any conscious desire, but all consciousness is born from it. The Change gives itself up to all, but it never exhausts itself. It is the overflowing and unrestricted vitality of all that exists in the world. Nature is natural and spontaneous because of the Change. The way of the Change is known through what is natural. What is natural is spontaneous, for its inner essence is the Change.

II. Creation

Creation is a process in which the Change is externalized. It is a process of becoming. It is a process of transition into becoming from the Void, the matrix of all and none. The Void is the Change unrevealed. The Void is the changeless change, the Change undifferentiated. The Void is the formless form, which is beyond distinction. It is the potency where the poles of opposites are unrealized. It is not the absence of being but the affirmation of possible becoming. It is the seed of becoming. It is like an embryo, having all the potential becoming yet without having anything actual. Creation is the transition of this matrix into the actual process of becoming. In this transition the discrimination of yin from yang appears. The appearance of the polarities of yin and yang is the beginning of creation. With the interplay of these two opposites, harmony and order come into a process. It is the beginning of differentiation and procreation.

This process of becoming presupposes the generating power of the Change. The potency of this generation is in the timeless time, the undifferentiated time, that is eternal. This was the fullness of time when the transition from the Void or Nothingness to the process of becoming took place. Just like an embryo, it needs the fullness of time to actualize itself. It must be the right time or *kairos* when the

Void began its actual process of becoming. Because of this fullness of time, creation is not an accident. It is not an accidental explosion of the concentrated energy and mass at the zero point of time. Creation is the process of differentiation between the opposites at the fullness of time. The discrimination of yang from yin or light from darkness marks the beginning of becoming. This process of becoming through differentiation and discrimination continues even to our time. This process may come to a halt at a certain peak of its expansion and then begin to contract again. Expansion and contraction between the two poles of opposites are continual because of the Change.

The Change creates the world out of itself, but the world is not the Change. Creation is the expression of the self-giving nature of the Change. The Change generates itself to make the transition from the Void to the process of becoming possible. Thus creation is an expression of the very presence of the Change. The Change expresses itself selflessly in the process of becoming, because its very nature is to give itself in its manifestation. It gives itself freely without expecting to receive. Its regenerating power is overflowing and eternally productive. It never stops to change and to create the new out of the old. It is like the mother who gives her love to fulfill the insufficiency of her children. It is eternally productive but never exhausts itself. It is like the overflowing electricity which can be transformed into power and energy. The Change is compared with the regenerating power of electricity which refreshes all the world without exhausting itself. It gives a new life in the Spring, and a fresh look every morning. It gives the essence of beauty and wonder to the world of nature. It gives the birds to sing, flowers to smile, and trees to dance. The world is alive because of the Change. The world belongs to the Change, and the Change is not effective without it. The world has no right to claim anything as her own. People are not independent of the Change. We are the part of becoming. All belong to the becoming, the constant realization of the Change.

23

Man is made of the dust. He is from the ground. He is of nature. In him the Change is most pleased to dwell. He is the image of the Change, the innermost essence of all becomings. He senses the Change as his own essence, but he cannot possess it as his own. Thus man cannot be the Change, even though the Change is in him. Because the Change is in him, he is not separate from other creatures. He shares his existence with all things in his environment. His life is part of the whole which is in the process of becoming. His becoming, like all other becomings, is governed by the opposite poles of birth and death. Between these two poles of opposites the process of growth and decay takes place. Birth is the initiation of growth and death is the utmost point of decay. With death a new life begins and the old ends. With birth the old becomes a new life and the new begins to change to the old. Thus birth and death are not in conflict but in a complementary relationship. Death is not only the end of life but also the beginning of new life. Everything, including the life of man, must reverse itself when it reaches its utmost degree. Death is both the end and the beginning of life. Birth is also the beginning of the new and the end of the old. Thus death and birth are one in two different poles of process. They are one in the Change, where there is no differentiation of existence.

Man is not essentially different from other creatures. He is *essentially* one with trees, grass, stones, animals, and all other forms of existence in the world. Regardless of their forms of manifestation they share the same essence, the very presence of the Change. Man shares the same ancestor with other creatures. This common ancestor is the Change itself. In this respect, all the creatures are brothers to one another. However, man is an honored creature among other creatures. In him is given the power to represent the Change in other creatures. The sign of this deputation is sealed in the image of the Change, the quality of his consciousness to know the way of the Change. Knowing the way of the Change more than other creatures, man is capable of leadership in the world. A good leader does not dominate but co-ordinates his followers. He does not oppress his followers, but liberates them. Thus man as a leader is not given any right to kill or oppress other creatures for his own glory. He is a deputy of the Change. He must not act as if he is the Change. Trees have the right to exist in the world. Stones have the right to be in the world. They are created to *be* in the world. What is created to *be* has a right to be. Man does not have the right to destroy them completely, for they were created to be in the world. Anything that is created has the right to be in the world. Creation presupposes existence. Thus all creatures are sacred, for the Change is the source of the sacred. Man is created to be an agent of the Change which is the way of harmony but not the way of conflict. To conquer nature is to conquer his own self. To preserve nature is to preserve his own body. The universe is an extension of his body, and his body is the extension of the Change. He must learn how to empathize with the remotest part of his own self, extending thousands of miles from his nerve center. Man is given the power to rule the world as well as the power to rule his own body. The power to rule is not the power to destroy. The ruler is not separated from the ruled. The ruler is a part of the ruled, and the ruled is a part of the ruler. They are essentially inseparable in principle. Thus to rule the world means to be ruled by the Change. To lead the world means to be led by the Change, which essentially leads the world. Man rules and sustains the world, so that he may be also ruled and maintained by the world. Thus man must rule others as if he is ruled, and lead them as though he is led.

The pollution of nature is the pollution of our own body. The water is the symbol of our blood, the air of our breath, and the soil of our flesh. The universe is an extension of man. Man is a microcosm of the universe. When the water is contaminated, our blood is also poisoned. When the air is polluted, our heart is heavy with breath. When the soil is polluted, our body is also defiled in the same manner.

The pollution of nature hampers the process of becoming. It will eventually stop the process of becoming. The process may come to a halt when the pollution reaches its utmost degree. Then the Change will eventually return to its primordial stage, the Change that is changeless. Pollution is then man's symbolic rebellion against the Change. It is man's attempt to halt the natural cause of the Change. But the Change will regenerate again to actualize the process of becoming. Pollution becomes a means for the process of decay, but never for the destruction of the Change. Man cannot destroy the environment completely without destroying himself. The destruction of nature is not an end of the Change but the end of man. The Change will begin a new cycle of process for the renewal of the world. Thus the Change will continue forever.

Man is *unique* not because of his essential quality but because of his existential quality, which is his acquisitiveness. He is created to be in the likeness of the Change. His existential quality is not identical but similar to the quality of the Change. It is then the *existential analogy,* the image of the Change, which makes man different from other creatures. His acquisitive quality of the Change makes him creative. The capacity of his creativity derives from the intrinsic quality of the Change, which is a creative potency. Thus man's power to create is external because its power is derived from the created. The uniqueness of man is then to re-create something out of the created. His re-creativity makes his externalization possible. The process of re-creativity which man makes is not a natural process of change. The external changes by the power of recreativity are unnatural, but the inner changes by the Change are natural. The inner changes are authentic, but the external changes which man makes are copies of the inner changes that the Change makes. Man's way of changes is then analogous with the way of the Change. This analogy of creative change between man and the Change is the image of the Change, which makes man unique among all other creatures. The great tragedy results when the external change which man possesses is not in harmony with the inner change which the Change makes. It is the external change which must conform to the inner change, which is inherent to all things. To be in harmony with his inner change, the very presence of the Change in him, is to be united with the Change. In the unity, the external change which man makes and the inner change which the Change makes are inseparable. They become one in two different manifestations. This harmonious union of the external change and the inner change in man is the highest goal of mankind.

III. Sin

Man is unique in his existential creativity, but he is *peculiar* among other creatures in the misuse of his unique quality. This peculiarity is called sin. Sin is not a substance, but a form of relationship in the process of becoming. It results when man's acquisitive quality is in conflict with the way of the Change, the inner quality of his existence. Sin is then man's estrangement of his existence from his inner essence of becoming. It is the blind assertion of his existence as his own essence. It is essentially the disharmony of existence and essence. It is his undue emphasis on the power of his re-creativity as the basis of all changes. It is the failure to know that his power of re-creativity is relative to the power of Creativity in the Change. It is to claim his own re-creativity as the absolute. Sin is a tendency toward making the relative absolute.

Sin is the assertation of *either* his existence *or* his essence. Sin is the separation of existence from essence. It is the separation of the objective self from the subjective self. It is the separation of the outer self from the inward self. These kinds of separations create the dichotomy between the counterpoles of human nature. The symbolic separation between them is expressed clearly in the story of the fall. Their harmonious union is broken in the fall, and the result is in conflict. The fall of man is the beginning of his acquisitive power to dominate his inward process of change. Thus the fall is not the sign of weakness, but the sign of strength for man's creative assertion. It is not the symbol falling down from above, but the symbol rising upward from the depth of his inwardness. It is the process of externalization of his power from his inner essence. Thus the root of sin is a willful disharmony in man through the assertion of his external power over his inner strength.

Sin is an attempt to *be* rather than to become. Sin results from man's desire to stop the process of becoming and to make it the state of being. It is man's assertion to stop the Change from changing; it is, then, man's revolt against the Change. An evidence of sin is a desire to be young forever. This desire to be young is an expression of sin. It is the desire to *be* rather than to become. Man does not want to be old because of sin. It is unnatural to stop the course of the changing process. Man's unnaturalness comes from his sin. What is natural is the way of the Change, and what is unnatural is the way of sin. Because of sin, man wants to stop the natural process of change. Sin takes the form of security in the world of relativity. Man's search for security in the relative world of change is the subtle form of sin. Thus institutions, associations, insurances, and all other forms of organizations become the instruments of sin. Every form of civilization is then the byproduct of man's sin, his being unnatural.

Civilization is a necessary evil, for its root is in man's sin. It is necessary, for it has become a means of human life. The coming of civilization is symbolized in the City of Babel, the city which revolted by creating a tower reaching to heaven. This symbol of civilization is a byproduct of man's unnatural inclination: man's desire to be the owner of the earth and to take the place of the Change. Scientific technology is man's adaptation of the way of the Change to create what is unnatural and unchanging. Medical science is man's adaptation of the way of the Change to control the natural course of life as much as possible. It is a result of man's desire to stop the Change in himself. Man wants to live forever without adhering to the process of becoming. Civilization is a counter-movement of the Change. It is the byproduct of man's acquisitiveness, which is contrary to the spontaneity of the Change. A key to civilization is a sophistication, which is to make man unnatural in the process of socialization. Through the process of socialization man comes to accept the unnatural as if it were natural. Thus civilization is the counterpart of the primordial way of life. The unnatural structure which civilization has built becomes the counterpole of the natural order of the universe. It is a means of man's intrusion into nature. Civilization is built on the ashes of the dying nature. Yet the ashes are the foundations of civilization. Thus the conquest of nature is also the destruction of the foundations on which our civilization is placed. Sin then brings the end to both civilization and nature together. It will destroy all but the Change itself, which will return to its primordial stage.

An institution is a cluster of sin. It is an instrument of unnatural process. It is a means of de-personalization. It uses the conventional drugs to anesthetize people, to separate them from their freedom. It promises the security of being, but it does not know that being is an illusion of becoming. The security based on the state of being does not endure, for everything is in the process of becoming. All the institutions will fall by the power of the Change, and people will seek their security in nature, the eternal home of becoming. Nature is the real home of free man and the field of his spontaneous activity. Those who rest their security on the structure of institutions are prisoners of their own creations. They live life in the illusion of being. They seek security within the walls but the walls cannot stand for them forever. Those who are free don't seek security in institutions. Those who are secure don't have to depend on the power of institutions. Thus those who are free from the institutional powers are indeed the liberators from sin.

The consequence of sin is an alienation of the outward

self from the inward self of man. The story of Adam is the story of man in our time. Because of sin, man is afraid of his inner voice, calling to him, "Where are you?" The voice is no longer his own, but strange and fearful to him. It is the voice of his own innermost essence, but it seems to come from someone else. He has to run away from his own voice calling. However far he may run, the voice is still heard, for it comes from his inner self. His life is the life of running away. The life of sin is the life of escaping from himself. His outward self is in conflict with his inner self. He is divided in an unreconcilable dualism. One runs away and another follows; one hides and another seeks. The perfect harmony is broken. He is fragmented. Sin brought a war within him. Man fights against himself. That is the predicament of modern man, the man of civilization, the man of institutions, the man of sophistication, and the man of sin.

Sin caused Adam to leave the Garden of Eden, the symbol of perfect harmony and peace. It was sin that threw him out from the perfect harmony of nature. He was in conflict with nature. Sin creates the broken relationship between man and nature. His environment becomes a hostile enemy, and he becomes no longer a part of nature. The very evidence of this conflict manifests itself in the sense of shame, the shame of the naked body, the natural body. Man has to cover his natural self with fig leaves, which separate him from nature. He has to wear something to separate himself from the natural environment. He cannot accept his own body as a part of the natural universe. He is not natural enough to be in nature. Nature becomes unnatural to him and a threat to him. It becomes an enemy against whom he has to fight back for his life. The enmity between nature and man begins here. The war between man and nature has started. Either man must conquer nature or nature must conquer him. In this war, man has produced a superior weapon, the weapon of scientific technology. With it he is able to overcome nature. Nature is gradually conquered and subdued by man. Now man does not have to run away from nature. He has overcome the fear of nature through scientific technology. He establishes his kingdom on the corpse of nature. But he soon realizes that his kingdom does not endure without the assistance of nature. His victory is an illusion. He has won the war, but he has been defeated in reality. The war he has fought is the war against himself. He has destroyed nature, the extension of his real self, the real home of his presence. That is the tragedy of man's fall!

IV. Faith and Reason

The knowledge of discrimination between good and evil is born out of the tragic consequences of man's fall. It is the fruit which opens man's eyes to see things discriminately. Now, everything in the world is seen in terms of dichotomy and conflict. Everything is to be classified as *either* good *or* evil. Things of opposite characters are in conflict rather than complementary. This dichotomy between good and evil prevails in all dimensions of existence. Everything has to be categorized according to this sharp dichotomy. Things are either right or wrong, either white or black, either cold or warm, either for or against, and so on. Nothing can come between these counterpoles of discrimination. An ability to discriminate between these poles becomes the basis of logical thinking, the seedbed of all intellectual and scientific developments. This rational category of an "either-or" way of thinking is a product of sin. Everything must be subject to the court of this kind of rational process. Anything that does not adhere to this kind of rational category has been denied its reality. The way of perverted thinking, that is, the "either-or" way of thinking, becomes the judge of all things because of sin. Even the ultimate truth has to come under the judgment of this rational court. That is the tragedy!

The knowledge of the undifferentiated whole, the knowledge of man before the fall, is decried as foolish. The all-comprehending reality of "both-and" thinking is humiliated and becomes the object of mockery because of sin. Any truth which is not objectified is to be rejected, because sin is an objectification of self. However, the real essence of knowledge lies in a new man who stands before Adam, the man of sin. The knowledge of new man is the knowledge before the fall, before the absolute discrimination between good and evil. To see things in conflict is to see them as existential appearances only. Thus it is our sin that makes us cling to the outward appearance. To think of our external appearance more than our inner disposition is an expression of sin. Sin splits man's outward and inward thoughts. In reality they are inseparable. To see them as a unity is, in a way, to restore the normal vision of human knowledge. This unity is possible in faith.

Faith is the knowledge before the fall, the knowledge of undifferentiation between subject and object. It is the knowledge of wholeness, the knowledge of both "I-Thou" and "I-It." Reason is then the knowledge after the fall, the knowledge of partiality, the knowledge of either "I-Thou" or "I-It." The knowledge of "I-Thou" is possible because of the intuitive reason, while the knowledge of "I-It" is possible because of the critical and analytical reason. The former knowledge deals with subjectivity alone, while the latter knowledge deals with objectivity alone. Faith must overcome the distinction between subjective and objective knowledge. Faith is both subjective and objective at the same time. It is then both personal and impersonal, but reason is either personal alone or impersonal alone. Faith uses the category of "both-and," while reason uses the category of "either-or." Thus faith is not a counterpart of reason. Faith transcends the dichotomy of opposites, which exists in reason. Faith is complementarity of opposites, while reason is their conflict. Faith responds to the wholeness of others indiscriminately, while reason reacts to the partiality of others discriminately. Faith reconciles the differences, but reason differentiates the undifferentiated. Thus faith is inclusive of reason.

If faith is the knowledge before the fall, its origin must be in the innermost essence of man, the Change. On the other hand, reason has its origin in man's sin, for its knowledge is given at the fall. Then, reason is born from faith because of the fall. Faith must have had a potential for reason, for the latter is the estrangement of the former. Faith, therefore, is an inclusion of reason and reason is the separation of faith. Because faith is the knowledge before the fall, it is prior to reason, which came after the fall. Thus reason presupposes faith, and faith realizes itself in reason because of man's sin. Reason always depends on faith. It is a realization of faith through man's sin. Thus faith is more than a mere subjective reality. Faith is both subjective and objective reality at the same time. It is the undifferentiated knowledge of both. Reason is the differentiated knowledge of them in an absolute sense. It is either subjective or objective, but it cannot be both of them at the same time. Faith deals with the process of becoming in which both the subjective and objective are not differentiated. Reason deals with the state of being in which both of them are clearly differentiated. Faith is a dynamic category, while reason is a static one. Faith recognizes reality in the process of change, while reason acknowledges it in the object of being. Faith becomes reason when the opposites are irreconcilable. Reason becomes faith when the opposites are united together. When reason changes to faith, man's dichotomy between his outward self and inward self is overcome. Faith is the union of the opposites, while reason is the separation of them. Thus to transform from faith to reason or from reason to faith is nothing but to unite or separate the opposite poles of man in the process of change. The union and separation or the harmony and disharmony between man's inward and outward self in the process of change ultimately determine the outcome of both faith and reason.

The ultimate is symbolized in the category of faith, the

category of "both-and" thinking. All penultimate matters can come under the category of reason, the category of "either-or" thinking. Faith alone deals with the ultimate reality, which is both the Change and Changlessness. Faith is not excluded in dealing with the matters of the phenomenal world, because it is the background of reason. Since faith is the source of reason, everything that is symbolized by reason comes under the domain of faith. People love the unambiguity and precision of distinctions, because they like reason alone without faith. To separate reason from its source, faith, is an expression of sin. Those who love reason alone detach themselves from the process of the Change and create the illusions of the unchanging world. Reason analyzes and discriminates becomings as if they are beings. Thus the rational process without faith fails to express the reality of the world. Faith expresses the reality as a whole, because of the category of "both-and" thinking. Reason without faith deals with a partial reality, because it is a category of exclusive thinking. Reason is real only in relation to faith, for it expresses the aspect of wholeness. Reason is an analytical tool to discriminate one from another within the totality of being or becoming. Faith, on the other hand, deals with the dimension of totality and wholeness of becoming. Thus, faith is the all-embracing, all-penetrating, and all-comprehending category of all becomings. Because of this universal category of knowledge, faith is a means of understanding the reality of the Change.

V. Salvation

The goal of every religion is the transformation of an "either-or" way of thinking to a "both-and" way of thinking, that is, the transition from a reasoning process to a faith-filled process. In this transition, man experiences transcendence. This is a salvation experience, the experience of totality from that of fragmentation. This experience transcends the partiality and discrimination of the world. It is the experience of wholeness and unity, the experience of realizing the Change in himself. This kind of experience is comprehended only in faith, the category of totality and undifferentiated wholeness. It cannot be expressed in the words of discrimination and analysis. Words imprison him in their definitions and conceptions. But faith, which transcends the conceptual words and ideas, liberates man from the illusion of them. In the transition from an "either-or" to a "both-and" way of thinking, man experiences emancipation from the imprisonment of conventional words and ideas, which are ordered and selected by the activity of reason. In this transition he is liberated from the deep-seated root of one-sidedness and a sectarian way of thinking. It is an experience of peace and harmony in his mind. The ultimate conflict and enmity between the opposite poles are gone. The war between the opposing forces is settled. There is no longer a feeling of either victory or defeat in mind.

Nothing is in dichotomy; everything is in harmony. All the opposites are now complementary to make the whole complete. In him, extrinsic and intrinsic, subject and object, or existential and essential self complement each other for a peaceful co-existence.

Man can attain harmony and peace when he gives up the peculiarity of his existence. He has to give up the unnatural tendency, which makes him peculiar from other creatures. In other words, he has to give up his desire to *be* rather than to become. The false security built on the state of being must be eliminated. He must throw himself unconditionally into the process of becoming. The transition from the "either-or" to the "both-and" way of thinking comes only when he makes a total commitment to the Change. It is "thy will be done." By renouncing the sense of superiority over nature he can make a transition from the "either-or" to the "both-and" way of thinking. The transition comes only when he gives up the idea of domination of one over the other. Unless he gives up the competitive spirit, he cannot experience peace and harmony. To give up the peculiarity of man is to renounce the weapon of conquest. When this weapon is eliminated, the real harmony between nature and man is feasible. Man then becomes natural from unnatural. He becomes part of nature, because he is of nature. He is reconciled with nature. He realizes that everything has a right to exist in the world. He can see things as they are. He finds more closeness to the natural than the created. He knows how to appreciate the wonder of nature. He can assist nature, and nature can assist him. The man of peace and harmony with nature is not lonely, for he is a part of the universe. He senses the whole universe in himself. He can now talk to trees, mountains, and stones, and they talk back to him naturally. He can share his feelings with animals and insects. He can enjoy the music of nature and understand the voice of silence. The wind can communicate its feelings by penetrating deep into his heart, and he can recognize the presence of its emotion. Flowers can smile at him, and he can sense their affection.

Everything becomes part of his life, because he is part of everything. Nothing can be separated from the Change, which becomes the foundation of everything. Each has different talents to fulfill the wonderful harmony in the process of becoming. Everything is indispensable for the whole possible. Some give themselves to others. Others receive them for the sake of the whole. Man becomes a part of giving and receiving to complete the harmonious process of becoming.

Being a part of this process man finds the Change in himself. It is the experience of rediscovery of the Change in him. The Change is not found somewhere outside of him, but within himself. It is neither the search of man for the Change nor the search of the Change for man. The Change is found when man becomes true to his real self. To be one with his inner essence is to be in unity with the Change, and to be with the process of the Change is to be in harmony with all things. To be one with his innermost becoming is the highest goal of all his aspirations.

The transition from the "either-or" to the "both-and" way of thinking, that is, the process of salvation, is not realized by the way of action. It is the way of non-action. Man's action produces attachment to his unnatural inclination. Any effort that he makes by himself is unnatural. Thus the way of man's harmony with nature is to be without action. There is no need to be anxious about tomorrow; it will be taken care of by itself. To think in terms of a "both-and" way is to think nothing, to see nothing, and to do nothing. By the cessation of his external activities, the Change is not interrupted. Then, nature will take care of him in its own course. Let not his heart be troubled, for the Change is in him to change as he ought to become. Any effort that he makes is a hindrance to the process of the Change. "Be still and you shall know that you are of the Change!" Activism is the enemy of the Change. The changes which man initiates are the counter-movements of the Change. The best way for him to behave is to be totally receptive to the Change. "It is not I who changes, but the

Change that changes me." The inaction of man provides in him the action of the Change, and his action provides in him the counteraction of the Change. Thus non-action is the way to transform the reason-oriented to the faith-oriented person.

Every effort that the Church makes is a counteraction to her own master. Her effort will help to strengthen the power of institutionalism, which is the enemy of the Change. Every action she makes promotes conventionalism, which binds her people to the structure of the past. Every action she takes intensifies the conflict between the sacred and the secular. Activism is the enemy of religion. Activity makes the muscles of organization too tense. The tense muscle produces nothing but anger and frustration. Let her muscles be relaxed! Let her action be of the action of the Change! Let the sacred be also the secular, and the secular be the sacred! Let not their differences be in conflict! The secular is necessary for the sacred, and the sacred needs the secular. The non-effort of the Church alone can eliminate this dichotomy. For both the secular and the sacred are of the Change. The harmonious co-existence between them is possible when they are not interfered with.

Every thought which man produces entangles him in the logic of the "either-or" category. Every action he makes gives him a desire to cling to the state of being. Every effort he makes creates in him an ambition to perform. Ambition creates competition, competition creates conflict, and conflict destroys the natural course of becoming. Non-action is the way of an authentic man. When he is not active, the Change is active in him. The act which the Change initiates is natural and spontaneous, and the thought which the Change makes is within the "both-and" way of thinking. To be an authentic man, the man of the Change, is to be like the child who bases his action and thought on the Change. That is why Jesus said that man must be like a child to enter the kingdom of heaven. The symbol of a child is the symbol of inaction and dependence. It is the symbol of indiscrimination and unadulteration. Thus to be like a child is to be a natural and faith-oriented person.

Silence is the voice of the Change. The Change speaks to man in silence. As Elijah said, "The Lord was not in the wind; and after the wind an earthquake, but the Lord was not in the earthquake; and after the earthquake a fire, but the Lord was not in the fire; and after the fire a still small voice."[1] The small voice is a voice of silence. Silence is the voice of all voices and the background of all sounds. The Change is not in the shouting voice of preachers. The Change is not found in the sound of Gospel songs. It is not in the loud voice of pastoral prayers. The Change is found in silence. In silence alone the Change communicates the depth of its mystery. The works of the Change are too subtle to produce a sound. It is too beautiful to be Church music. Silence transcends all the forms of voices. It expresses what the sound cannot do. In silence we are one with the Change. Silence is the voice of our inner becoming, the depth of all sounds in the world. When the water is deep, it is silent. When it is shallow, it makes noise. So the Change, the depth of all becoming, is in silence. In silence the Change meets man and man hears it. In silence man finds his true self. In silence he hears his inner voice, the voice of the Change.

Man finds the Change when he is lonely. Loneliness is a means of knowing the mystery of the Change. The Change moves into the heart of a lonely man. Loneliness opens the depth of his heart, so that the Change can penetrate into it. Loneliness comes from one's detachment from conventionalism. It is an isolation of oneself from the unnatural involvement. Thus in loneliness he receives the sympathy of nature. In loneliness he can look into his own self. In loneliness he becomes one with the Change. In loneliness Jesus overcame the power of temptation. In loneliness Buddha was enlightened. In loneliness man is naked to see his own self, the true Self. Thus loneliness is the quality of sainthood and prophecy. In loneliness he is helpless to assert his own will over the natural course of change. In

---

[1] I Kings 19:11-12.

41

loneliness he can ask the Change to control his life. Loneliness is the sentiment of detachment, which makes the Change feel at home. It is a simple feeling, the feeling of the unsophisticated, the natural feeling, which creates the emotional harmony between man and the Change. In this simple feeling man is naked, shorn of his cultural mask. He becomes the plain man, untouched with civilization. Man's loneliness is a sense of returning to the original home of his real self. It is a nostalgia of his innermost becoming, the Change itself in him.

The plain and unsophisticated self is manifest in the attitude of modesty. Humility is the disposition of the Change. Like the running water, the Change moves along the lowly places. Water never flows upward, so the Change never is revealed to the man of pride. One's arrogance is like a fortress which stops the natural course of the Change. The wall of pride alienates him from nature. The man of modesty is open to all the possibilities of the Change. Modesty is the attitude of yielding oneself to the course of nature; it is giving up his unnatural inclination and being willing to abide in the process of becoming. In humility, man reconciles himself to nature. In it the Change is pleased to reveal itself. In humility Jesus won the favor of people. In it man is exalted, for the Change moves into the loneliness of the man whose attitude is modesty.

Tragedy is the opportunity of the Change. It is the destruction of all values on which man depends. It is the annihilation of his hope in the state of being. It is the nakedness of self. In tragedy man has nothing to rely on. He is helpless. He is alone without power, without wealth, without pride, without honor, without selfishness, and without any claim to recognition. He is completely detached from the sense of security which has protected him from nature. Tragedy radically rips him from all external things. He is disclosed completely, so that he can see his genuine self as it is. Tragedy penetrates into the depth of the human heart. It vibrates in the last layer of the human emotion. It reaches into the rock bottom of the heart. It strikes the

42

innermost self of man. Thus in tragedy man finds the real self of his own becoming. To find his own self is to find the Change in him. To find the Change in him is to be natural. To be natural is to be in harmony with all things. He becomes one with nature. Dichotomy between the opposites is gone. There is no conflict between them. They are in complementarity to each other. That is why it is possible to "love an enemy," that is, to love the opposite. The enemy is no longer an enemy but a counterpart of the whole. The enemy is not in conflict but in complementarity. The man of tragedy is a victim of the enemy, but he is the victor of the conflict. He is defeated but has won the war. He is helpless but he is natural. The defeated becomes natural, and the natural makes all complementary. The enemy becomes his friend and an essential part of the harmonious process of becoming. In tragedy man is transformed from conflict to complementarity, from unnatural to natural, from self-reliance to self-affirmation and from self-alienation to self-union. Thus tragedy is an opportunity for man to find his real self and the Change in him.

The man who has realized the Change is a changed man, who alone has the authentic existence. When his inwardness is realized, he is enlightened. He is no longer the man of conflict between the opposites. He has overcome the powers of dualism. He is free from the "either-or" way of thinking. He who is changed is the man of enlightenment. He sees his inner light which is no longer in struggle with his outward appearance. He is free from the inner struggle and finds peace in himself. He is a changed man, because his will to be is overcome. The will to be brings conflict but the will to become makes complementarity. The will to be is struggle, but the will to become is peace and tranquility. A changed man is no longer in the state of being but in the process of becoming, because he wills to become. To be part of becoming, the changed man is no longer a man between the two powers of being and non-being, but a man above them. He overcomes the conflict and reduces it to a creative process of becoming. As part of the creative proc-

43

ess, he also becomes part of the Change. He no longer feels the cleavage between subject and object in himself. He is at peace, for his subject and object are one and undifferentiated. He acts according to nature, because he is part of the Change which controls nature. His mind is constant and his disposition is steady. He thinks spontaneously, for he does not restrain in his thinking. His thought is a reflection of the Change. His mind is pure and undefiled. It is like the shining mirror which reflects the very moment of the Change. He does not have any passion or desire to be himself. He does not have the desire to possess others, but always gives himself for others. He gives himself, for he is also the receiver of others in the rounded whole. His giving is also receiving. He is what he is because of others, and others are possible because of his presence. He sees the world not as his object; he sees it as his own extension. The world is then both subject and object at the same time. He thinks everything in terms of the "both-and" category. He does not separate the essence from the existence of the world. When he sees a tree, for example, he sees also its treeness, the subject of tree. The subject of tree is the realization of the Change, which is also his own subject. Thus he and tree are different as objects but same as subjects. They are one in their essence, because the Change is in everything. Because of this oneness, they are deeply involved in each other. They are in empathy with one another. He can feel that the tree is one with his own extension. The tree also senses that man is part of its own expression. In this mutual empathy the genuine appreciation of each other's existence is possible. Everything in the world shares its intrinsic nature in a deepest sense. The man of change feels not only the mutual fellowship but the mutual kinship existing in all things. This realization of cosmic consciousness comes only to those who are realized by the Change.

The man who has been realized by the Change is free from the desire to be unnatural. He is pure in his existence. Purity of his existence is in its transparency. It is a non-restraining and non-resisting presence of the Change. It is the negation of self-assertion. It is completely yielding himself to the Change. The purity of existence means an annihilation of his desire to stop the course of natural change. His purity makes his existence nothing. It is devoid of any desire to differentiate his outward appearance from his inward essence. He does not have any desire to externalize himself when his inwardness is perfectly realized. He exists, but his existence is his essence. Thus his purity is an existential nothingness. The existential nothingness is also the essential allness. As Jesus said, "Blessed are the pure in heart, for they shall see God." It is his purity to see the divine, the essential allness. In purity the essence and existence are one, as inward and outward self are united. In purity of heart, man's existence is also his essence, and his essence is also his existence. In this undifferentiated process of becoming, the perfect realization of the Change is possible.

The man who has been realized by the Change can transcend the category of his own existence. He can transcend it because of his essential allness. He has to exist to be transcendent. His transcendence is conditioned by his immanence, the existence of himself in the world. He is immanent, because he is in the process of becoming. He is transcendent, because his inwardness is of the Change. In him, both the changed and the Change itself are brought together. He shares both the immanence and the transcendence of the Change. His transcendence is relative to his essential harmony with the Change, and his immanence is relative to his existential harmony with the Change manifested in the world. When the Change is perfectly realized, he is both transcendent and immanent. He is both the divine, the inner presence of the Change, and human being, the external manifestation of the Change. He is fully divine, because he is completely transcendent. He is fully human, because he is completely immanent. In the perfect realization of the Change both divinity and humanity are not differentiated. In this undifferentiated process of becoming the prototype of man, the perfect man who is also the perfect divine, is symbolized in the enlightened person, who is also Jesus Christ.

VI. Incarnation

Incarnation is a process of manifestation. It is a process in which the divine becomes man, that is, the Change manifests itself in the world. Incarnation is not man's realization of the Change. It is the realization of the Change in man. Thus Incarnation is the counterpole of salvation. The former begins with the Change and ends with human existence, while the latter begins with human existence and ends with the Change itself. The former moves from essence to existence, while the latter moves from existence to essence. This dialectical movement between incarnation and salvation makes the entire process of change possible. They are complementary for the wholeness of changing process. One is necessary for the other. Thus salvation presupposes incarnation, and incarnation is necessary for salvation. They are one in two different realizations.

Incarnation begins with the Change, the essence of all that is. It is said, "The Word became flesh." The Word is a symbol of the Change, and flesh is the symbol of human existence. Thus the Change becomes man, rather than man becoming the Change. It begins with the Change and ends with man. However, incarnation is not the coming of the Change in man or in other forms of existence. The Change does not come or go. The divine does not come from outside or go outside of man. The Change which is also the divine is within man and within all the processes of becoming. It is the ground of all becomings and the depth of all existences. It is the inner Self of all things in the universe. Thus "The Change becomes man" means the inner revelation, that is the disclosure of the inner self in the external self. The disclosure of the inner self in man is possible because of existential nothingness. In other words, incarnation is the transparency of the inner self in human existence. It is an outward realization of the inward presence of the Change. It is the process of externalization of the Change in all things. Therefore, incarnation is not an intrusion of the divine in man. It is not the coming of the divine from above. Rather it is the process of becoming from below toward above and from inside toward outside. Incarnation takes place in everything, for everything has its inward self, the presence of the Change, which is in the process of realization in a visible form of existence.

Incarnation and creation are mutually inclusive. Incarnation signifies the intrinsic process of creation. Creation is the external manifestation of incarnation, and incarnation is the internal basis of creation. Incarnation is a direct process but creation is an indirect process of manifestation. Both of them are none other than the manifestations of the same essence, the Change itself. Both of them are mutually dependent on each other. Without incarnation, creation is not complete. Without creation, incarnation is not possible. Their relationship is clearly illustrated in the story of creation. The world is created through the Word, the inner presence of the Change, which is the basis of all creative process. The Word which is spoken at creation is the spirit and breath of all things. It is the inward life of all creative manifestations. The Change is incarnated when the world is in the process of becoming. Everything that exists in the world is an incarnation of the Change. Thus creation and incarnation are inseparable. Creation is the existential manifestation of the Change, while incarnation is the essential manifestation of the Change. Thus creation is an external basis of incarnation, and incarnation is the

47

internal basis of creation. They are mutually interdependent to complete the process of becoming.

The most perfect incarnation of the Change makes an authentic man possible. This authentic man is known by many names, such as the Christ, the Buddha, and the Krishna. The authentic man is the archetype of all men and the highest symbol of existence. In the authentic man, the Change is perfectly manifest. He is then the *final* mode of incarnation. In him the Change becomes final. The inner presence of the Change is realized in him ultimately. The Change is realized in all forms of manifestation, but it is realized in him ultimately. This ultimacy of incarnation makes the authentic man different from other men and other creatures. Because of this ultimacy he becomes the symbol of archetypal man.

The authentic man as the most perfect realization of the Change also points to the fulfillment of every creative process. In him the dichotomy between existence and essence is completely overcome. In him the Change itself and the changed are one. The conflict between the unnatural desire of man and the natural trend of the Change is not existing. In him incarnation is creation and creation is also incarnation at the same time. His external self is so perfectly coordinated to his internal self that there is no real distinction between them. In him, dichotomy becomes complementarity and conflict becomes harmony. It is neither the domination of the Change over the changed nor the domination of the changed over the Change. It is the perfect harmony between the Change and the changed or between the divine and the human. In him the perfect realization of *both* his spirit *and* his body, *both* his transcendence *and* his immanence, *both* his inwardness *and* his outwardness and *both* his inner presence of the Change *and* the outer manifestation of it are possible at the same time. This perfect harmony in him is possible because of the perfect realization of the *both-and* category at the same time. In other words, the perfect harmony between the opposites is possible because of their perfect realization of the Change. He is an authentic

48

man, because he is *both* authentic person *and* authentic divine simultaneously. This perfect harmony with perfect realization of the Change in all things is a focus to which the whole creative process of the world is moving. Creation does not move toward the complete domination of the Change over the created. The creative process moves toward the fuller realization of the Change. When the process of the Change is fully realized in all things, including both personal and impersonal or both animate and inanimate, then the realm of the Change is to be fulfilled. The perfect realization of the Change in the world does not mean the rule of the Change over the world. It is the perfect realization of the Change which makes the perfection of the changed possible. It is also the perfect realization of the divine which makes the perfect realization of man possible. The perfect realization of transcendence makes the perfect realization of immanence possible. The former is necessary for the latter and the latter is essential for the former. One cannot dominate the other. Both of them are perfectly realized by the Change. When the Change and the changed are perfectly realized, the perfect harmony will come. Thus the perfect realm of the Change is the fullest realization of both the divine and human, inwardness and outwardness, essence and existence, and heaven and earth. The goal of creative process is the fulfillment of all opposites in the perfect realm of the Change. The authentic man as the perfect realization of the Change and the changed is a symbol of this cosmic harmony. He is the symbolic presence of the perfect realm of the Change.

The authentic man has, then, a cosmic significance to all things in the universe. He is a cosmic reconciler, for he represents the focus toward which all creative process moves. He gives the vision of reconciliation between the opposites. The authentic man is the symbol of peacemaker among all things, among men, among the animates and among the inanimates. He is the symbol of reconciliation between personal and impersonal existences. He is the focal point of both personal and impersonal beings. He transcends the

49

dichotomy between personal and impersonal categories. Thus, he is the first born of all creation, the focus of all creative activities in the world. He is the center of the living as well as the dead. He is also it and it is also he in the authentic person, because he is known in the "both-and" category. He is the first born of the living as well as the dead. Thus in him the living is dead and the dead is also living. In him all the opposites are undifferentiated and united together. Because of this undifferentiated continuum in him, his divinity is also his humanity and his humanity is also his divinity. He is the Change which is also the changed at the same time. Thus in him all things are united together in perfection and in harmony. He is the cosmic reconciler of all things.

The authentic man as the perfect incarnation of the Change means also the mediator of all things in the universe. He is most of all a mediator between the inward and outward self of man. Without him the Change is not carried out to the world, for he is the focal point of all creative process. He is the mediator, because he is the inspiration of all perfect harmony and the focus toward which every power of creation moves. He is compared with the navel of the body through which the unborn baby draws the nourishment from his mother. In him everything comes together. In him all dimensions of existence are overcome. Everything comes together in him. He is the point of meeting for all and the point of departure for all. Everything has to be in him, from him, and toward him, for he is the mediator of all possibilities. He is the focal point of everything that exists and shall exist. He is the beginning and the ending of all things. In him the beginning is the ending and the ending is also the beginning, for they are not differentiated. Thus, "in him all things hold together."[1]

---

[1] Col. 1:17.

VII. Crucifixion and Resurrection

Crucifixion means the negation of life, while resurrection means the reaffirmation of life. Man does not have one without the other, for reaffirmation presupposes negation. Resurrection is inseparable from crucifixion. In crucifixion life was negated, but it was also the way of reaffirming life. Without negation there is no affirmation. If resurrection is impossible without crucifixion, crucifixion is necessary for resurrection. Thus crucifixion is the way of the Change toward the reaffirmation of life. Both resurrection and crucifixion are sharply contrasted with each other. The former deals with the destruction of life and the latter with the renewal of it. Nevertheless, they are inseparably united in the authentic man, the man of perfect realization of the Change. In him they are not in conflict, but in complementarity. His resurrection is not the conquest of his crucifixion, but the fulfillment of it. Resurrection is not the victory of life, but the fulfillment of life. It does not replace death, but fulfills it. Death is the end of life, but resurrection is the restoration of that life. Thus they are not in conflict, but complementary to each other. In the authentic man, both death and life as well as crucifixion and resurrection are united. In him they are inseparable.

Resurrection is also crucifixion. They are not two different things. They are inseparably one, because they deal with the same thing. Crucifixion deals with the depth of life and resurrection with the depth of death. Both of them deal with the depth of existence. They are united in the depth of all things. Crucifixion reaches the depth of life through descending, while resurrection rises up from the depth through ascending. Both of them take place within the process of becoming, within man, within things in themselves. Resurrection is the process of rising from inner self to the outer self, while crucifixion is the process of falling down from the outer self to the inner self. They are inner experiences of all existence in different directions. Thus they are one in two different forms of manifestation.

Resurrection and crucifixion are two poles of existence in all things. Resurrection is the ultimate symbol of renewal of life, crucifixion is that of the renewal of death. Spring is the symbol of cosmic resurrection, and winter is the symbol of cosmic crucifixion. Spring does not come without winter, and winter is always followed by spring. In spring everything renews its life, and in winter everything withdraws its life back to the depth of its existence. Resurrection is the morning of day and crucifixion is the shady side of life. The former is positive and the latter is negative. The former is yang and the latter is yin. In all things there are yin and yang. Thus in all things there are resurrection and crucifixion. Every day man dies and rises again. Both resurrection and crucifixion are the counterpoles, but are complementary to each other. Their relation is like that of the wind with a flower. The wind is hostile to the gentle leaves of the flower, but is necessary for its propagation. Without the wind, rain does not come and the flower does not grow. Crucifixion is hostile to resurrection, but without the former the latter is not possible. One cannot exist without the other.

Crucifixion is a countermovement of the Change, while resurrection is the restoration of changing process. Crucifixion attempts to change the becoming to being. It is an attempt to destroy the process of change. On the other hand, resurrection is the revival of that process of becoming. It attempts to restore the pulse of the Change. Thus in crucifixion the natural process changes to unnatural, while in resurrection the unnatural process changes to natural. Through the interaction of these two opposites, the process of the eternal change is maintained in all things.

The Change becomes the victim of crucifixion, but it revives again through resurrection. In crucifixion, man takes the power of the Change in his own hands. In resurrection man has to give up the Change. Through resurrection man is no longer a master of the Change. Man loses the power to control the Change. The Change resumes its process through resurrection. Resurrection is, then, a key to the Change. The process of change was once stopped by crucifixion, but resumes again through resurrection. Crucifixion is a divine eclipse, while resurrection is a human eclipse. In crucifixion the sun stops shining. It was dark when Jesus was crucified. In crucifixion the Change ceased to function. The Sun did not shine on that day. The light was darkened at crucifixion. At resurrection the sun again shines in the sky. It is the morning, the rising sun above the sky. Even though the process of change is interrupted by crucifixion, it is the very nature of the Change. Interruption is a necessary part of resumption, just as rest is essential for action. Thus crucifixion is necessary for resurrection, because it is the way of the Change. Crucifixion and resurrection are the matrices of all changing processes. The crucifixion of Jesus was the finality of all negations, while the resurrection of Jesus was the ultimate affirmation of all process of becoming. Jesus was the authentic man, the archetypal man, whose crucifixion and resurrection represent the ultimate symbols of negation and affirmation of the whole process of becoming.

In the interim between crucifixion and resurrection lies the abyss of unconsciousness. The abysmal danger must be passed to find a real life. The life before crucifixion is the life of illusion and the life of the unnatural. It is a life in illusion, ignorance, and self-imprisonment. It is the life of agony and search for real life. It is the life of reason and

53

entanglement. It is the life of discrimination and conflict. But the life after crucifixion is the life of non-ego, the life of unconsciousness. It is the life of nothingness, which prepares the life of allness. It is the annihilation of external power which makes man unnatural and the destruction of desire which clings to the world of civilization. The life after resurrection is a real life. It is the life of liberty and wholesomeness. It is the life of peace and harmony. It is the life of abundance and joy. The life after resurrection is to be born again, born from the deepest abyss of danger. This is an experience of new becoming—the old is renewed by the rebirth experience of resurrection. He who is born again never experiences crucifixion again. He is no longer in the process of becoming, but a becoming itself. He is no longer the manifestation of the Change, but he has the inner presence of the Change in himself. He is one with the Change. He is no longer subject to illusion and the cycle of birth and death. He is part of eternal becoming. In this life, man is fully realized by his innermost presence of the Change. He becomes an authentic man, who is perfectly realized by the Change, the eternal Change in the midst of the changing world.

VIII. Liberation and Freedom

One of the distinctive marks of new life is liberation. Liberation is a mark of an authentic man. Liberation is possible through the authentication of self through the perfect realization of the Change. The most appropriate title for Jesus as the authentic man is the liberator. He is first of all a liberator of himself from the power of enslavement. Crucifixion means to strip off from himself the power of sin. It is in fact the act of liberating himself from that power that put him on the cross. In crucifixion he ceases his own existence so that he may be free from the enslavement. It is an act of detachment through his own death. He annihilates himself from the presence of slavery. For the liberation he has to give up himself. He becomes the victim of the power from which he wants liberation. Liberty is then as costly as life itself. He did not liberate himself through the oppression of others. He yielded himself totally to aggressors. He did not resist the power of sin. He bore the cross willingly. As he said, "Blessed are those who are persecuted for righteousness' sake." His real strength was in his weakness. His yielding was the way of attaining his goal. This was the mysterious work of the Change. In the annihilation of his existence the power of sin could not take hold of him. Thus he attained liberation through detachment.

The authentic existence of man is negated by crucifixion

but is reaffirmed by resurrection. In crucifixion the authentic man escapes from the power of sin, but in resurrection he rises up from the abysmal death. Resurrection is the affirmation of liberation. In it he is no longer detached, but has attached himself to the life, the new life of liberation. His attachment to his innermost presence of the Change is the underlying power of resurrection. In resurrection he is no longer the old man, but an authentic man who is renewed through the presence of the Change. He becomes the perfect realization of the Change itself. Because of this perfect realization he becomes natural. He is attached to what is natural and detached from what is unnatural. Thus liberty includes both detachment and attachment. Detachment alone cannot make man free. Liberty is more than a mere detachment from the power of slavery. Without attachment the liberty is incomplete. The failure of the pietistic idea of liberation is to take this idea of attachments too seriously. Detachment is necessary for attachment, and attachment is possible because of detachment. Both detachment from what is unnatural and attachment to what is natural are essential for liberation.

The liberty of Jesus as the archetype of all changing process is a basis for our liberty. The same process of detachment and attachment is necessary for us to be liberated. Jesus as the authentic man is the pioneer of our salvation, said Paul. He is the way of our liberation, for he is the focal point of the realization of the Change in the world. As he has done, we must be crucified by the power of sin. We have to annihilate ourselves from the power which makes us unnatural. We must not fight it back. It creates conflict, which is not the way of the Change. It is not to win the war against the power of enslavement, but to get away from its chain. The way of liberation is detachment of our existence through death. We must die to be liberated. How can we die? Do we have to die to be liberated? Paul suggests that we must die in baptism so that we may rise again. We must die in baptism to detach ourselves from the power of sin and rise in it to attach ourselves to the real life. Thus crucifixion and resurrection are represented in the symbol of baptism. Baptism is a symbolic act of detachment and attachment. We don't have to fight our enemy back. We can get away from him through baptism. In baptism we are deeply immersed in the water. We detach ourselves totally from the power of evil into the abysmal depth of water. Immersing ourselves into the water we are stripped of the power of enslavement and cleansed from the pollution of sin, and rise again with newness and purity of life. Immersion represents our way of descending into the abysmal depth, and rising from the water represents our way of ascending from the depth. The real meaning of baptism must be the experience of both crucifixion and resurrection. Its result must be the life of liberation. Baptism, therefore, has been from early days intended for the liberation of man from sin, the original sin. Baptism is a gateway for liberty in a symbolic sense.

The process of detachment and attachment is also the way of liberty for the cosmos. When light is overshadowed by darkness, it does not fight back. Light yields itself to darkness, so that the latter might be in control of the world. Light has to extinguish itself in the night. It descends deep into the bottom of shadow. Light yields itself to the power of darkness, for it is the way of the Change. Yielding is a means of attaining the goal. Its strength lies in its weakness. When light yields itself completely to darkness, it begins to expand again. The complete immersion of light in darkness represents crucifixion, and its rising from it represents resurrection. Light rises from the abysmal darkness and renews its brightness. This is the process of attachment to its own essence. Thus the process of detachment and attachment through the dying and rising is the way of liberty for the day. Winter represents the season of dying and spring the season of rising. The death of the old makes the detachment from life possible. The rise of the new makes the attachment to life real. The process of change according to detachment and attachment makes liberty feasible. Liberty is to be a part of the changing process. Thus it is not

57

possible in the state of unchanging being.

Freedom is possible because of liberty. Freedom is the quality of new life. It makes the new life different from the old. Freedom is not self-control or autonomy. It does not mean to be self. It is not doing as one wills. It is the quality which makes renewal possible. It has the quality of creativity. It is not a quality of being, but of becoming. It is possible only in the process of becoming. Anything that is static hinders freedom. Without renewal there is no freedom at all. The renewal is possible only in the process of change. Thus outside of the changing process there is no freedom. Freedom is a creative process of detachment and attachment. It is the creative quality of liberty. It is born in liberty, but liberty is sustained by it. Both freedom and liberty are one, but two different attributes. Liberty is the background of freedom and freedom is the foreground of liberty. To separate one from the other is to dismiss all together.

Freedom is expressed in a spontaneous process. Anything that is not spontaneous cannot be free. Spontaneity is a natural process. What is natural must be spontaneous also. Thus freedom is always accompanied by a natural process of becoming. A free man acts according to his own nature. He who is natural is always free to himself. On the other hand, he who has an inclination to be unnatural is not free. That is why sin takes our freedom away. However, freedom is more than the liberation from sin. It is a process in which creative activities take place. Freedom is seen in the running water, following its natural course without any hesitation. It is expressed in the process of a growing tree. It is expressed in all other processes of becoming. Freedom is, therefore, the quality of the Change. To be in the process of the Change is to be free indeed.

Freedom is an expression of faith. The man of faith is free but the man of reason is bound to himself. Faith is a category of both transcendence and immanence, while reason is that of immanence only. To be free is to be unbound by the logic of reasoning. Freedom is an expression in the *both-and* way of thinking, the category of faith. The man of faith is free because he thinks in this *both-and* category. The man of reason is bound to the category of *either-or*. He cannot transcend the laws of logical analysis and conceptualizations of ideas. But the man of faith transcends them because of the undifferentiated whole. This dimension of transcendence is the quality of freedom. Faith has this extra dimension, which reason does not have. Thus freedom is an expression of faith. He who does not have faith is not free to himself. To be free is to be faithful.

Freedom is known when man is not conscious of himself. When he is conscious of himself, he is not free from himself. Man is a prisoner of his own consciousness. He is imprisoned by his illusions and desires to stop the process of becoming. The man whose mind is preoccupied with himself is not free. Thus the man who is not free cannot relate himself fully to others. He cannot have genuine empathy with others. He cannot give himself to others, because he clings to himself. On the other hand, a free man can give himself fully to others, so that he is conscious of others rather than himself. Freedom is active when his self-consciousness is not. Freedom comes when one's mind is empty.

Freedom is an expression of harmonious unity. Freedom is possible only in a harmonious unity. Disharmony and conflict produce unnatural inclinations which enslave man. Freedom cannot exist in the midst of conflict and disorder. Thus a real freedom is found only in harmony and unity. The real freedom does not impose one's will upon the will of others. Freedom does not come through the domination of one over another. A genuine freedom is possible when the opposites are complementary to each other. Freedom is not possible in isolation. Privacy is not freedom, but self-imprisonment. The man who is free is open to others. His openness to others is the mark of a free person. The man who is really free to himself is the one who has opened himself to the Change. He who changes according to the process of the Change is free. He who wants to retain the old is not free. A free man is a man of becoming, but the slave is a man of being. The man of being is self-conscious, while the man of becoming is selfless. He who is conscious of himself cannot be conscious of others. Thus freedom is found when man loses himself in the process of becoming. In this process, freedom provides an opportunity for him to realize his own inward presence of the Change.

IX. Anxiety

Anxiety is freedom unrealized. When freedom is not fully realized, anxiety arises. Freedom is based on the harmony of opposites, but anxiety is produced by the unfulfilled harmony. Anxiety is then based on the confusion of roles between the opposites. Their relationship is neither in conflict nor are they complementary to each other. In anxiety there is a possibility of freedom. The actualization of this freedom comes through the clarification of roles between the counterparts. The confusion of roles is apparent in the life of civilization. In the home there is a confusion of roles between husband and wife, between parents and children, and between brothers and sisters. In society the roles of male and female and of the old and the young are not clear. In schools the roles of students and teachers are not clearly defined. We see the confusion of roles apparent in all areas of life. That is why it is the generation of anxiety, that is, the generation of the confusion of roles. Since anxiety is a byproduct of the confusing roles of the opposites, it is not restricted to human beings. Anxiety is inherent to everything, including animals, trees, stones, and even space and time. Since everything has the interplay of yin and yang, the possibility of anxiety is inherent in all things. When the roles of yin and yang are confused, anxiety is produced. Yin is to be yin and yang is to be yang in their relationship. They are not to be altered in a harmonious relationship. When their function is ambiguous, disruption arises. This disruption manifests itself as a form of anxiety.

Anxiety is possibility unrealized. When one's possibility is not totally realized, he has anxiety. The possibility can be either within his own reach or beyond it. Anxiety is an incompletion of his possibility. For the completion of this possibility within the given situation, anxiety may act either as a creative or as a destructive process. When it is creative, it can produce a new possibility. When it is destructive, the possibility changes to impossibility. The creative possibility that anxiety produces is the expansion of existing possibility. Thus it creates more anxiety without solution. The destructive anxiety brings the anxiety to an end, but brings the end of hope. It is the beginning of despair. On the other hand, the creative anxiety is the beginning of hope but never fulfills the new possibility. It is a process of tension maintained within the boundaries of interplay between the counterparts. On the other hand, the destructive anxiety arises when the internal tension is too great to maintain the boundaries of their interaction. The creative anxiety builds the restless society of our time, while the destructive anxiety creates conflict and alienation. Thus anxiety, whether it is either creative or destructive, is the underguarding strength of our civilization.

Anxiety is the state of being unrealized. It is an attempt to maintain the state of being in the process of becoming. It is the constant awareness of one's existence being threatened by becoming. It is a possibility of losing his security built on his existence. The possibility of threat is a constant reminder of his uncertainty and restlessness. The state of being which he wants to maintain changes to the process of becoming, but he wants to cling to it. Thus the being to which he holds is not real, so that it will never be realized. This is the dilemma of man's desire and the reality of the Change. It is, then, his ignorance to the reality of the Change. He wants to be in the state of being, which is not possible in reality. Thus he never actualizes his desire. Be-

62

cause of his failure to realize his desire, he becomes anxious. He is insecure because of becoming. This insecurity is a basis for his anxiety. One of the chief causes of anxiety is the desire to be young forever. To be young means to be in the state of being, rather than in the process of becoming. No matter how hard he tries to be young, he grows old. He cannot stay young forever. This failure to stop the process of becoming is the cause of anxiety.

Anxiety is the absolute unrealized. Anxiety is an attempt to take hold of the absolute in the world of relativity. Man knows his finitude but wants to be infinite. He knows he is relative, but seeks to be absolute. He knows that he cannot be perfect, but he wants to be perfect. He knows that the absolute is beyond his possibility, but he cannot stop to think of being an absolute. He knows that he is a creature, but wants to be the creator. What he knows is in conflict with what he wants to become. In reality both of them are one and inseparable. What is relative is absolute, and what is absolute is also relative. The failure of this realization produces the desire to seek for the absolute outside of the world of relativity. He never actualizes the absolute because he thinks that it is apart from the relative. The failure of this realization produces anxiety. Thus the primary cause for anxiety is ignorance, the ignorance of the true relationship between the world of relativity and absolute. Anxiety for death, for example, is the failure to realize that the absolute is also relative. Man seeks for immortality, even though his mortality is immortal. This search for immortality is not found in the outside of his mortality or death. He fails to recognize that both life and death are inclusive. The life and death are relative, and the absolute is found in the relative also. If man knows that his relativity is also his absolute, he does not seek the absolute. The desire to seek the absolute, in spite of absoluteness in his essence, creates anxiety. This anxiety is the anxiety of illusion and ignorance.

Anxiety is reality unrealized. Man seeks for reality in an either-or way of thinking, but it is not in this category of thinking. Reality is in the both-and way of thinking. Thus the man of reason seeks reality, but it is not fully realized in him. He is a man of anxiety. On the other hand, the man of faith realizes reality in the wholeness of the both-and category. Thus he doesn't have anxiety. The man of faith is free from anxiety, because he transcends the distinction between failure and success, between life and death, between good and bad, between being and non-being, between absolute and relative, between saints and sinners, or between the Change and the Changeless. In his both-and way of thinking he is in the undifferentiated continuum. But the man of discriminative and analytical reason fails to see this wholeness of reality. He sees the opposites in conflict rather than as complementary. Thus he fails to reconcile the dichotomy he has created. This failure is a cause of his anxiety.

When fear becomes its extreme, despair comes. Fear moves into a new dimension of threat to his existence. Despair is the renunciation of his self-affirmation completely to the object of fear. Despair is more than fear. It is a complete surrender to that towards which fear is aroused. It is an end of struggle to assert his own existence. It is a willingness to admit his failure. Despair is the end of hope, so that it is also the beginning of it. Despair is to give up his unnatural assertion to be because of becoming. It is then also the beginning of becoming. It is both the end and beginning of hope. It is the end of the old, but the beginning of new life. Thus despair is the opportunity of the Change. It is a means of enlightenment and realization of true self. Despair is man's way to admit his finiteness to nature. In despair he sees that he is also part of nature. In despair he completely strips himself off from his own illusion to be. He does not have anything to claim for his own possession.

Anxiety comes from the failure of realization, but fear comes from the realization of failure. Fear is more than the intensive form of anxiety. It is a new dimension of threat to one's self-affirmation. Anxiety does not realize the object of its threat, but fear realizes it. Anxiety does not have a direction, but fear has the direction toward which it moves. Fear includes a cognitive element, while anxiety does not. Fear is caused by the object of threat immediately available, while anxiety is caused by the expectation of it. Man is anxious for the unknown, but he is afraid when he knows the direction of the unknown. Thus anxiety is the initial stage of threat to his existence. Fear is the next stage of this threat. The final stage of it is despair. He does not have any pride to be better than nature. He does not have anything to protect and secure his own existence. He is completely naked in despair. In despair he is truly alone by himself. He does not depend on any other than what he is and is to become. He has to wait for the power of the Change to do anything. The Change becomes his ruler. In this pure and undefiled moment of existence man finds himself, the true self, the inner essence of his own existence, that is, the presence of the Change itself. He realizes that he is of the Change. Despair may bring his life to the end, but the end of life is the beginning of new life. Therefore, it is the despair that eventually solves the problems of fear and anxiety.

X. Love

The foundation of the changed life is love. Love is not a character or an attribute, but the very nature of the changed life. Love is the totality of man's response to the Change. That is why Jesus has commanded us to love others with all our heart, all our mind, and all our strength. Love is the whole process of becoming. It is compared with the water in the river. It is the water that makes the river possible. Thus it is the love which makes the changed life possible. That is precisely why Paul said love is the greatest of all.

It is a grave mistake to separate love into its different kinds. There are basically two shades of love; the self-giving and self-receiving love. They are not different kinds, but different shades or textures of love. The self-giving love is not independent from the self-receiving love, because they are one in essence. The only difference between them is the direction of movement. Both of them have the *self* in common. The self-giving love moves from inner to the outer self, while the self-receiving love moves from the outer to the inner self. The self-giving love is the outward movement of life and the self-receiving love is the inward movement of life. They are the same love in two different directions. The self-giving love is incomplete by itself. It always *presupposes* the self-receiving love. That is precisely why Jesus commanded to love others as yourself. To love others implies the self-giving love, and to love yourself implies the self-receiving love. Thus to love others means to love oneself. The self-giving love implies the self-receiving love at the same time. The self-giving love is self-negation, while the self-receiving love is self-affirmation. Just as crucifixion is inseparable from resurrection, the self-giving love cannot be separated from the self-receiving love. The self-negation is inseparable from the self-affirmation. Thus the self-giving love is also the self-receiving love.

Is love not different? Is the love of man different from the love of the divine? Is the spiritual love different from physical love? They are essentially one. They are love, the inner essence of harmonious union, the complementarity of the opposites. They are different only in their manifestations. The perfect love is the perfect union and perfect fulfillment of mutual needs. The perfect union of man and woman is as perfect a love as man's union with the divine. Love is known differently because of the different intensities of harmony and union. There is no qualitative distinction between the love of man and the love of the divine. In all manifestations of love there are different shades or levels of perfection. Love itself is one and the same. The love with which man loves the divine is the same love with which he loves his neighbours. They are different forms or manifestations of the same love. Love is one—the wholeness, totality, that is not to be divided. Love is the inner essence of all harmony and union, which is maintained by the complementarity of the opposites. Perfect love is the perfection of mutual harmony and union between these opposites. Since love is one, it is the undifferentiated continuum of the opposites. Love does not differentiate or discriminate, for it is the wholeness. It is the most inclusive and mutually empathetic. Love is the universal process of harmonious becoming. It is one in many different manifestations.

Love is primarily the inner trend of harmonious unity. It makes the inner harmony of all things possible. Things tend to unite together because of love. The nature of love

67

is not to bring the opposites into conflict and disorder, but into complementary and harmonious union. Love has its own polarity—the self-giving love and the self-receiving love. The self-giving love corresponds to yang, and the self-receiving love to yin. Yang completes yin because of the self-giving love, and yin completes yang because of the self-receiving love. Just as yin and yang are complementary to each other, these two poles of love are also complementary to each other. It is the self-giving love that gives the self and the self-receiving love that receives the self. Through the interplay of giving and receiving self the harmonious unity is maintained. It is the self-giving love that completes the self-receiving love, and the self-receiving love completes the self-giving love. One is not better than the other. The self-giving love is creative, while the self-receiving love is receptive. Thus the interplay of these two is necessary for the harmonious existence of all becomings.

The love of God is not the self-giving love only. His love is not complete if it is one-sided. God's self-giving love expects the self-receiving love of his counterpart, the world. It is well stated that giving is also receiving. The giving-love is also the receiving-love. There is no self-receiving love without the self-giving love. The self-giving love of Jesus is not complete without our self-receiving love. The self-giving love of Jesus as the Christ presupposes the self-receiving love of ours. Thus we cannot talk of one without the other. When the self-giving love of Jesus is without the self-receiving love of the world, love becomes incomplete love, the love unfulfilled, that is, suffering. Thus his love, the unfulfilled love, is not a perfect love, but suffering. His love is then not an ideal love, but the love of the cross, the love unfulfilled. This unfulfilled love of Jesus as the authentic man is not love in reality. Love involves both the receiving and giving self. Thus when we speak of the love of Jesus as the authentic man, we must also speak of our response to him. We cannot speak either of the former alone without the latter, or of the latter alone without the former.

The Change works in love. It directs the world through love, the inner essence of harmony and unity. The Change without love is chaos and conflict. It is the love that makes the Change complementary and harmonious. The orderly and unifying process of becoming is possible because of love. Love is also creative in the process of becoming. The Change does not repeat the old but renews the old because of love. The creative process of the world is possible because of the interplay of the giving and receiving love. Thus the self-giving and the self-receiving loves are the procreative powers of yin and yang, the primary category of all production and reproduction. Because of this intrinsic power of creativity of all things, Paul remarks that nothing can be separated from this love.

Love deals with the union of opposites, not the union of the same. The harmonious union of the same is not possible. The union of the same is an unreal love and an illusion. Love in all forms of expression is the complementarity of the opposites. The homosexual behavior is often condemned because the same is unlovable. Love does not express itself in the relationship of the same. Man can love others because they are not identical. When both the lover and the beloved are identical, there is no complementary relationship possible. Since love presupposes the complementary relationship, it is possible only when the lover is different from the beloved. Thus Confucius was careful in defining the counterparts in human behaviors. He defined the five different counterparts in life; between husband and wife, parents and children, elder brother and younger brother, elder friend and younger friend, and between the subject and ruler. In this kind of relationship, the relationship of counterparts, love is effectively maintained. If love means the interplay of giving and receiving self, how can the interplay take place when both parties are identical? It is, then, not an accident that nothing in the world is identical. Everything is different and relative in time and space. That is why the process of the Change continues and love is active everywhere.

Love is in a process of becoming. It is not in a state of being. It is in a constant interplay of giving and receiving self. Through the constant giving and receiving self, it can fulfill the lack within the wholeness. Love fulfills the needs of each other. It fulfills the other by the self-giving and fulfills the lack of his own by the self-receiving love. Through this mutually fulfilling interplay the Change is constantly operating. Love is more than the sacrifice of one at the expense of the other. One's sacrifice is for the fulfillment of others, and the fulfillment of others is in return for the fulfillment of his. Love deals with the whole process of becoming, the process of the giving and the receiving self. The lover is also the beloved in this process of wholeness. In love the lover and the beloved are not separated. They are united together. Thus to love others is to love oneself. Love is inclusive of all differences, for it is the whole process of becoming.

Love is not limited to human beings only. If love is in the whole process of becoming, it must be applicable to all, for all are in the process of becoming. Thus love is active in all things. Love is possible between man and animals, between man and tree, man and air, man and mountain, mountain and river, river and stone, etc. In all dimensions of existence love is active, for love makes the creative process of becoming possible. Since love deals with the harmonious union between the counterparts, it is not possible to love unless they are in empathy. Without empathy, the total participation of one in the other as his own, love is not effective. As long as they are mutually participant totally in each other, they can love. Man and tree, for example, are in love if they are mutually participating totally to each other. In this total and mutual participation, the harmonious union between tree and man takes place. In this harmonious union the giving and receiving are exchanged freely and fully. The mutual giving and receiving take place only when they are not identical in the world, love can be effective in all, for love is the essence of all harmonious union and the way of complementarity to each other's needs.

Love is spontaneous. The process which is not spontaneous is not love. Love moves like the flowing water and the air of the open field. Love does not act upon the premeditated attempt. Love is a spontaneous response to the beloved. It is therefore direct and intuitive. It is not purely rational. It is not motivated out of rational process. No one makes love, but love can make man love others. Love never makes him conscious of himself. It is natural. To be in the process of natural movement man is not conscious of his own self. To be unconscious of his own existence is to be in harmonious union with the one whom he loves. In the process of love one does not notice his own presence. He becomes the part of the beloved, for he is totally participating in the beloved. Because love is spontaneous, the moment of unconscious self is possible. In this moment of love man finds the void, the undifferentiated continuum. In this void man realizes himself. He becomes one with the inner presence of the Change, which is also the essence of the beloved. Thus in every moment of genuine love the moment of unconscious self is found. In this moment man can experience a new life, the life of the changed and wholeness.

The outward manifestation of love is justice. Justice is not something independent of love. Love is the inner essence of harmony and unity, while justice is the outer manifestation of harmony and peace. Love is then the inward presence of justice, and justice is the outward expression of love. Love is the basis for justice and justice sustains love. Love is the basic disposition to the order and justice. Love is an inward inclination inherent in all things, while justice is the outward manifestation of it in the actual life situation. Justice is an externalization of it in the actual process of becoming. Love is interested in the mutual participation to give and receive themselves. Justice is interested in mutual protection and in providing the possible situation for the interplay of giving and receiving. Justice is objective and impersonal, but love is personal and subjective. Justice makes use of reason as a means of rectification, while love makes use of faith as a means of understanding. Justice makes use of law to enforce it, love makes use of grace to penetrate it. Justice is impatient, but love is patient. Justice is cold, but love is warm. Justice is necessary because of conflict and disorder, but the order and harmony is the spontaneous creation of love. Justice tends to be static, while love is dynamic. Justice tends to be formalistic, love to be natural. Even though they are different, they are inseparable. Justice and love are one in two different forms of manifestation. Love is the inner essence, while justice is external presence of harmony. Both are two sides of one coin.

Love makes freedom possible. Freedom is actualized by love. Freedom does not make love possible, but it makes love active. Love is active in freedom. Those who love are free to themselves. Freedom is both the product and means of love. Freedom is the means by which a loving relationship is established, for love operates in freedom. Freedom is the servant of love. Where there is love there is also freedom. Love does not work where there is no possibility of freedom. Love is where freedom is. Love without freedom is love ineffective. Freedom without love is unreal freedom. Thus freedom and love go hand in hand. The effectiveness of love is relative to that of freedom. Love is like electricity. It cannot be effective without its conductor, freedom. Thus both love and freedom are complementary to each other. One cannot exist without the other. Love and justice are the bases for freedom, but they cannot be active without it. Love, justice, and freedom are mutually complementary to one another to make the whole process of becoming possible.

XI. Suffering

Suffering is love unrealized. When love, the inner essence
of all harmonious union, is incomplete, it realizes itself as
suffering. Love thus has the possibility of suffering. Suffering
is the incomplete love, the love unfulfilled, or the harmonious union unrealized. To love means to expect suffering, for love that is not complete is suffering. Suffering may
be caused by the struggle for love as well as by the apathy
to continue for love. The former is constructive suffering,
for it aims for perfection of loving relationship. The latter
is negative, for it is the beginning of disintegration of love
that has been established. The constructive suffering is creative toward the successful love, but the negative suffering
is destructive of the existing harmony. The constructive
suffering is a process toward the completion of love. It trains
for love to complete the harmony. Suffering is a school-
master who makes love perfect. Thus suffering is positive
as long as it becomes a means for love.

Suffering is also a process toward the destruction of the
loving relationship. When love begins to disintegrate itself,
suffering is born. This kind of negative suffering makes
love impossible. The disintegration of love makes suffering
hopeless. This hopeless struggle leads to the destruction of
all possibility. It will bring the end of all possibility, that
is also the beginning of new possibility. Thus the negative

73

suffering is the other pole of the positive suffering. The former moves from harmony to disharmony and the latter from disharmony to harmony. The latter leads to a successful love and the former leads to the destruction of existing love. Since the destruction of love is also the beginning of new love, both the destructive and constructive sufferings are one in two different directions.

Suffering is caused by the desire to be unnatural, the root of sin. It is this desire that stops the natural course of becoming. It attempts to interrupt the process of becoming. The Buddhist solves this problem by eliminating the unnatural inclination; the Christian attempts to solve it differently. He knows that suffering is a part of life. Thus he wants to solve it by transforming it to love, rather than eliminating it. Both Buddhist and Christian have approached it differently but arrived at the same place. The Buddhist eliminates the desire to be unnatural so that he finds the void, the unconscious moment of self, the moment in which love is perfected. The Christian transforms the struggle of the opposites to the harmonious union, where the moment of unconscious self is created, the perfection of love. One approaches it negatively, while the other positively. Both positive and negative approaches are one in two directions. Either way will meet together, for the two ends—positive and negative ends—are not separable.

Suffering is caused by the desire to stop the changing process rather than to be part of the world of relativity. The Buddhist fails to recognize that the process of becoming is real. It is not the being, but the becoming that stops suffering. The reality of the world is not in the state of being, but in the process of becoming. It is not the desire to cling to the relative world, but the desire to stop that relativity which causes our suffering. To be in the process of the Change is to be in harmony with nature and to be in the state of being is to be in suffering. Suffering is caused by one's ignorance of being able to assert his being in the process of becoming. This assertion to be in the face of

74

becoming creates the conflict of life. This conflict is a basis for suffering.

Suffering is love distorted. Suffering arises when the essence of harmony is distorted. The essential harmony is based on mutual giving and receiving of love. The distortion of this harmony is due to either disruption or the destruction of the mutual fulfillment. The disruption of harmonious union may be due to the failure of one to fulfill the other. When the self-giving love fails to fulfill the self-receiving love, it becomes suffering. When the self-receiving love fails to meet the needs of the self-giving love, it also becomes suffering. The counterparts of both the self-giving and self-receiving love must be mutually complementary to be in a harmonious union, a perfect love. The failure of one to do its part will result in suffering. The destruction of one creates suffering to its maximum. This kind of suffering is experienced when the beloved is lost. This extreme form of suffering becomes a form of grief. The suffering of Jesus as the authentic man is precisely his love extremely distorted. When the authentic man gave the self-giving love to the world, the world did not receive him with the self-receiving love. John recorded it very clearly when he said, "He was in the world, and the world was made through him, yet the world knew him not. He came to his home, and his own people received him not."[1] The world is the manifestation of his self-giving love. Yet, the world receives him not. The failure of reception by the world has created the suffering of the authentic man. His love was disrupted by the failure of his counterpart, the world. Thus the self-giving love is wounded. It is the innocent suffering, the love of the cross.

Suffering is proportioned to love. More suffering is possible when more love is available. To love more means to expect the possibility of more suffering. The loss of an intimate beloved creates great suffering because of great love. But the love of the unloved may never cause any suffering

---

[1] John 1:10-11.

75

at all. The intensity of suffering is proportioned to the intimacy of love. Some cannot love deeply, because of their fear for the possible outcome of the deeper suffering. Some may not love at all, in order to avoid suffering completely. Those who are afraid of possible suffering cannot love. Love and suffering are in an inseparable unity.

If the divine love is greater than the human love, divine suffering must be greater than human suffering. To deny the possibility of divine suffering is to deny the possibility of divine love altogether. God's love is also the possibility of God's suffering. It was the Greek view that denied the suffering of the divine. In the process of becoming the divine is part of this process. In this process the Change also shares the suffering of the changed. The Change is not separated from the changed. Thus in the process of becoming the divine also shares the same agony and suffering as well as the joy and happiness of mankind. To separate the divine from the human and the Change from the changed is to deny the process of becoming.

Suffering is the inner conflict created by the relationship between the self-giving and self-receiving love. Pain is the externalization of suffering. Pain deals with the immediate manifestation of suffering. It deals with sensation. On the other hand, suffering deals with the internal disharmony of relationship. Thus pain is not suffering, even though they are inseparably related to each other. However, pain is impossible to conceive without suffering. Both pain and suffering are mutually derivative. Pain becomes suffering and suffering becomes pain. The external disorder effects internal disorder, just as psychic maladjustment effects physical disease and vice versa. Just as the physical body is inseparable from the spiritual body, pain is not separable from suffering. Both pain and suffering are the products of disharmony and the conflict of opposites, even though they are manifested differently.

Suffering is not anxiety. Anxiety deals with the tension within the opposites, while suffering deals with the actual conflict between them. The tension between the opposing poles is not identical with the actual conflict between them. The former can become the actual form of conflict as well as the perfection of harmony. Tension is neither the conflict nor the harmony of the self-giving and self-receiving love. Thus anxiety is the initial stage of suffering. Anxiety comes from the confusion and frustration of the opposites, while suffering comes from the disruption and destruction of relationship between the opposites. In anxiety, an actual conflict is not yet realized. Thus anxiety is compared with a germinal situation, which is not yet realized in the actual process of becoming. Anxiety is then either unrealized suffering or unrealized love. It is thus intimately related with suffering and love, but still a distinctive form of process. They are not separated, but inter-related with one another. None of them is to be isolated from the others. The extreme form of suffering is manifested as grief, that of anxiety as despair. The former is the complete destruction of the complementary relationship, while the latter is the complete loss of hope for a possible harmony. Both of them are the end of the old and the beginning of new possibility. Grief is the beginning of new harmony and unity between the opposites, while despair is the beginning of new hope. They are similar, but not identical. Likewise, suffering and anxiety are similar but not the same thing. They are fundamentally dealing with the distortion of harmony, but phenomenologically different. Thus suffering and anxiety are essentially one, for they deal with the incomplete relationship of the opposites. They are existentially different, for they deal with the different situations of existence.

XII. Meaning and Hope

It is meaning which sustains life from suffering and pain. Meaning is not the achievement of goals; it is not the fulfillment of desires. It is more than a mere doing or success. Meaning is much more than a mere activity. It is that which makes the activity desirable. It is that which directs the activity. It is, then, the perspective toward which the achievement of goals is to be realized.

Meaning is more than the ability to control one's own affairs. It is not the possession of power. Meaning is something that makes possession real and significant. To control his own destiny is an affirmation of his existence, but not that of meaning. Meaning is more than the power of free choice. It is more than a self-control. It is something that motivates him to control his own destiny. Meaning is then deeper than the power itself. It makes power real and relevant. Meaning is compared with the seasoning which makes food tasty. The food that is not tasty is still a food, but meaningless. Thus meaning is something that makes one conscious of the inner presence of the Change in all things. It is that which makes things real.

Meaning is not dependent on the state of being. To be is meaningless. Meaning comes from the Change that changes all things. It is meaningful to change. It is meaningless to be the same forever. Meaning is something which makes it relative; it is not that which makes it secure. What is secure is meaningless, but what is relative is meaningful because of the Change. Anything that is meaningful is related to the Change. The things of the Change are relative. Thus meaning is found in relativity, which is also absolute, for relativity is the creation of the Change which is absolute.

Meaning is not found in the things that are external to themselves. It is not in the external manifestation of the Change. Rather it is in the inner presence of the Change in all things. Meaning is found in the inner harmony of all things, that is, love. Thus meaning is of love. What is of love is meaningful. Love makes things meaningful. Things that are meaningful must participate in love. To be in love is to be in harmony with the Change. Thus to be meaningful is to be one with the Change.

Meaning is found in the wholeness. What is fragmentary and partial is not meaningful. Meaning deals with the totality of things. To be meaningful is to be a part of the whole process of becoming. To participate in the process of becoming is to find meaning in life. Isolation from the changing process is the life of meaninglessness, and participation in the process of the Change is to find meaning in life. Meaning is not realized in the analytical and discriminative reasoning, but in the undifferentiated continuum of wholeness. To be meaningful is to see things as a whole. Thus meaning is expressed not in the rational category of the either-or but in the faith category of the both-and thinking. Meaning is known only to the man of faith.

Meaning sustains hope, and hope inspires meaning. Meaning attempts to integrate everything, while hope attempts to draw all things together in harmony. Meaning is not effective without hope, because hope is the object of meaning, and meaning is the subject of hope. Thus hope and meaning are one in two different manifestations. Hope without meaning is empty, and meaning without hope is dead. Both of them are inseparable.

Hope is directed to the future, but it deals with the present. Hope has its base on the past. Thus hope is inseparably related to the past, present, and future. To have hope means to have all different dimensions of time at the same time. Hope is the present directed toward the future, based on the past. To be in the moment of now is to have hope. Now is the boundary between the past and the future. Thus, to be in the present is to be in hope, to be in all dimensions of time. Because hope includes all dimensions of time, it draws all things together.

Hope is not a wish. Wish is illusion, while hope is real. Wish is based on the expectation which is not real. It is the unnatural desire to be in the future. It is fragmentary in character. It deals with one dimension of time only, the future dimension of time, that is a mere expectation. It does not deal with the wholeness of time. Thus wish is unreal. Hope, on the other hand, deals with the wholeness of time. Thus it is the reality of expectation.

Hope is promised in the process of becoming. It is not the expectation which is conditioned by the past and present. It rather conditions the present and the past. Hope is promised in the beginning. Thus hope is more than the fulfillment of the end. It is also the fulfillment of the beginning. Thus hope fulfills both the beginning and the ending. In hope there is no differentiation between the beginning and the end, between past and future, and between sin and salvation. Everything is to be consummated in hope. Hope is the promise that swallows up all things. In it the Change manifests itself fully in all things.

Hope is the inspiration of all becomings. It is like the light shining in the darkness to show the way to the journey of eternal becoming. Hope is not attainable, but it inspires all toward the attainment of their harmony with the Change. Hope is not the way, but it illuminates the way toward the goal of every becoming. It makes things aware of their participation in the wholeness of becoming. It draws them into the wholeness from their separations and isolations. In the journey of endless becoming the hope re-freshes the world to new strength. Hope does not disappoint us, but comforts us in the weary journey toward the eternal process of becoming.

XIII. Prayer

Hope is expressed in prayer. Prayer is a communication of hope between one's inner self and his outward self. Prayer without hope is not a prayer. In prayer, hope is shared mutually. Since hope is inclusive of all dimensions of time, in prayer the past, present, and future are brought together. This undifferentiated time is expressed in prayer because of hope. Prayer, therefore, is more than a mere conversation between the outward self and inward presence of the Change. Hope makes prayer effective, for it brings the communion of all times together. Because of this undifferentiated time, prayer deals with the future event which is brought into the moment of now by hope. The past sin is forgiven at the present moment of prayer, because the past becomes present reality through the presence of hope. Thus the essence of prayer is hope. Without hope prayer is not a prayer, but a mere gesture.

Prayer is more than a communication in hope. It includes a communion between the outward self and inward self in the presence of the Change. In prayer they are mutually participating in each other. This mutual participation is the empathy between the inwardness and outwardness of the presence of the Change. In empathy the inward presence of the Change is shared with the outward manifestation of the Change. In this mutual sharing through the empathic participation, the idea of covenant is at work. The concept of covenant is nothing but the complementary relationship between the inward and outward self which is made possible by the presence of the Change. In prayer, covenant is realized. In this covenant relationship the divine or the inner presence of the Change is active, while the human or the outward manifestation of the Change is receptive. The divine is yang and the human is yin. The divine is the self-giving love and human the self-receiving love. The self-giving love is fulfilled in the self-receiving love, and the self-receiving love is fulfilled in the self-giving love. Thus in prayer the mutual needs are to be fulfilled

The language of prayer is not the words of sound, but of silence. Silence is the sacred voice, the divine speech. Silence is mystery, which alone can convey more than all the words have combined. In silence, divine speaks and man listens. Thus man who prays to the divine must speak in silence. He must listen to him in silence. Man who prays with a loud voice does not know how to pray, but knows how to perform an arrogant rite before the audience. It was Jesus who criticized the hypocrites and pharisees who made a show to the public with a loud and long prayer. He told us to pray in silence. Real prayer is the prayer in silence; the language of prayer is the source of all languages. Divine and human minds are met in silence alone. Silence is a universal language, the language of secret, the language of inwardness.

Prayer must not be directed to heaven or to outside of the one who prays. It must be directed to his own inner self, the inner presence of the Change. The divine is not outside of man, but within him. Prayer is then directed to the one who prays. The proper attitude of prayer is the mood of concentration. An effective prayer comes from the concentration of oneself to the depth of his own existence. The communion between the divine and human, or between the outward and inward self is possible because of concentration. Concentration is to bring the outward and inward self together. It is a means to attain the undifferentiated whole by the isolation of outward from inward self. It is that which makes the real communion possible. In this real communion the self-giving and self-receiving love respond to each other to fulfill the hope.

Prayer is the communication of the Change between one's inward and outward self. Prayer is not confined to human beings. Everything that is of both the inward and outward expressions of the Change is capable of prayer. Since the language of prayer is silence, even animals and trees can pray as people do. Animals may pray in silence to the inner presence of the Change, even though we do not notice them. In silence every prayer must be "Thy will be done." It is a mistake to conclude that human beings alone can pray. It is human civilization that takes away the language of prayers. Prayer is not possible in the life of noisy civilization. Since silence is taken away by the ceaseless flow of electronic communication, there is no language to communicate the presence of the Change between the inward and outward self. The sacred language of nature, silence, is polluted by our civilization. The sacred language is conquered by the secular language, noise. Thus prayer in nature as well as in human beings is almost impossible. Civilization is the enemy of prayer.

Prayer is not confined to a particular period of time. Prayer is possible at all times. As long as the presence of the Change is communicated between one's inwardness and outwardness, prayer is in effect. As long as one is in union with the presence of the Change, he is in the mood of prayer. The perfect moment of prayer is in the moment when he is not conscious of his own self. In perfection of prayer he is in perfect communion with the Change, the divine reality. In this communion he is not conscious of his own existence. In the real prayer, the moment of void is created. In this moment of void alone all the needs are perfectly fulfilled through the interplay of the self-giving and self-receiving love. The experience of this void may come at any time. As long as he has that moment of void, he is in prayer.

84

Prayer is communication in communion, while meditation is communion in concentration. Both prayer and meditation deal with the communion, the total participation of counterparts for mutual fulfillment. Meditation aims at communion, which is the basis for communication. There is no communication of mutual understanding without communion. Since communion is of meditation, meditation is of prayer. Meditation is incomplete without prayer, and prayer is not possible without meditation. Meditation, which deals with the communion, is also communication, because communication is not real without meditation. Thus meditation is always followed by prayer. Prayer is also not a real prayer without meditation, for communication is possible because of meditation. Prayer is then the realization of meditation, and meditation is prayer unrealized. Thus both prayer and meditation are one in two different phenomena.

In meditation the spiritual and material selves are brought together. The method of concentration, or yoga, is not to reduce the physical body by the spiritual power, but to bring both of them in a harmonious union. Buddhists are more sensitive to the method of concentration than are Christians. They do not stress the extreme domination of one over the other, but the middle way. The middle way denies the domination of one over the other. It is the harmonious co-existence between the spirit and the body. It is also a Christian idea that the matter is as significant as the spirit. The underestimation of the matter is alien to the Judeo-Christian view of the world. Thus, in meditation, both the spirit and the matter are brought together in an undifferentiated continuum. In this continuum the mutual interaction between the spiritual and material aspects is possible. Thus in prayer the spirit can be transformed to matter. In prayer, the transformation of the intangible to the tangible expression is possible. That is why we pray for the blessings of material wealth in spirit. In prayer, both spirit and matter are inseparable. Thus they mutually influence each other.

85

XIV. Spirit

The spirit is the power of the Change, the power of inner self. Matter is the outward manifestation of the spirit. The spirit is not confined to a certain creature. It is not in living beings alone. It is in all things that are manifested in the form of existence. Since the Change is in all things, the spirit, the inner presence of the Change, is the essence of their existence. Even the darkness, for example, has its inward power, which complements the power of light. The inner power of darkness, that is, the spirit of darkness, is manifest in its darkness. He who is a slave of this power is afraid of darkness. Even the red has its inner power, the spirit of red color. A child who has been frightened by this spirit may find it difficult to overcome even in his later years. Everything has the spirit, the inner power of existence. The tangible manifestation of the spirit is the matter. Even the tree that we see is the manifestation of its inner essence. The spirit of tree often seduces artists and lovers of nature to reproduce it in the form of paintings, sculptures, or poems. It is the spirit of flowers that often moves the hearts of man and woman.

Everything we see is the manifestation of the spirit. Just like energy, the spirit is transferable to the material. There is a continuity between spirit and matter. Just as energy is mass in a given condition,[1] spirit is also matter in a certain situation. The continuity between energy and mass is analogous to the continuity between the spirit and matter. The real distinction between the spirit and matter is not in their essence but in their existence. They are essentially the same, but existentially different. Both of them result from the productivity of the Change, but they are manifested differently because of different conditions. Thus the spirit is the matter unrealized in the world, and the matter is the spirit realized. They are one, but two different forms of manifestation. Thus they are inseparable. To separate the spirit from the matter or the soul from the body is to deny both of them altogether. Whenever the spirit is, the matter is also. We cannot speak of one without the other.

The spirit, the power of inner essence, is the power of harmony and unity, this is also the power of love. Spirit is love empowered. Just as love is endowed in all things, the spirit is inherent in all. It is the spirit which makes the interplay of the self-giving and self-receiving love possible. The spirit without love is the power of the unnatural and the disharmony, and love without the spirit is the process of harmony unrealized. The spirit moves the process of becoming in order and in harmony because of love. Love is the power of life because of the spirit. It is the spirit which gives power to love, and it is love which gives to power the trend of harmony and union. Thus love which is not spirit is not the real love, the spirit which is not love is not the right spirit. Love and the spirit are inseparable.

The spirit deals with wholeness as well as concreteness. It is not fragmentary, but the totality of becoming. Because of its wholeness of becoming, it heals the broken humanity and the world. It mends the broken pieces together to make a whole, for it is the power of becoming and creativity. The spirit can break through the static institutionalism and provide it the possibility of a free and spontaneous process of becoming. Its spontaneity and creativity heal the frag-

---

[1] $E = MC^2$

mentary character of our civilization. It overcomes the dichotomy between subject and object, and brings the conflict to the complementarity of opposites. The spirit of Spring is the healing power of nature. The rise of new creation out of Winter expresses the spontaneous power of the Change. This new creativity is the spirit, the power of inner essence. The beauty in harmony and directness is the manifestation of this spirit in nature. The spirit overcomes the fragmentary inclinations and polarities and creates the process of grand harmony and peace.

The spirit overcomes the ambiguity of life. It is the power of conviction and confidence. Thus the spirit is expressed in faith. The either-or category of reason divides, but the both-and way of faith brings the separation into a harmonious whole. The spirit is the totality of becoming which is not to be classified in the analytical category of reasoning. It is the category of transcendence and infinite. The spirit belongs to the category of faith. The spirit of faith is not the ambiguity, but the conviction which involves the totality of self. Conviction is the participation of one's total self in the process of becoming. It is the spirit which makes this participation possible. The spirit is active in faith alone. That is why the man of faith is capable of knowing the work of the spirit.

The spirit overcomes the dichotomy between the secular and the sacred. The overcoming of the dichotomy does not mean to make the secular sacred, but merely to close the gap between them. The spirit brings the opposites closer in harmony and complementary relationship. The spirit heals the conflict and creates the harmonious whole. The sacred is the opposite of the secular, but they are not in conflict. It is the spirit which makes the complementary relationship between the secular and sacred possible. What is sacred belongs to the domain of the inner self and what is secular belongs to the domain of the outer self. Thus the sacred is an expression of essence and the secular is an expression of existence. Both the secular and the sacred are mutually complementary through the work of the spirit.

The spirit is the reconciler of the separated and the inner power of the Change in all things.

When the spiritual presence is realized in the community of people, it is called the community of faithful, or the Church. The Church is then the community of the spirit. It is created by the coming of the spirit into the midst of the people. This community of the spirit had existed even before the coming of Jesus as the authentic man. However, the community of the spirit is renewed through the renewal of life in resurrection. The resurrection of Jesus as the authentic man was the beginning of the Church renewed. In crucifixion, the old Church died and the new Church was born in resurrection. In resurrection, the old becomes a new community of people in spirit. It is returning to an original community through the renewal of the spirit. Crucifixion was the end of the cyclic change and the resurrection was the renewal of it. Thus crucifixion and resurrection are inseparable in the spirit and united in the community of believers. The Church is renewed through the renewal of spiritual presence. Resurrection is a revival of the spiritual presence in the community of people. Thus, the Church was not born at the resurrection of Jesus as the authentic man, but renewed by it.

The community of the spirit is in a process of becoming. It is called the people of pilgrimage—the people of journey toward the perfect becoming. It is infinitely becoming, because the perfect becoming is infinite. The process in which the community of the spirit abides moves according to the principle of change and transformation. It is not free from the process of growth and decay or the process of expansion and contraction. When it grows, it will decline. When it declines to its minimum, it will grow again to its maximum. It is a part of the process of change. It is the symbol for the eternal process of the Change. When the community of the spirit is in a state of being rather than in the process of becoming, it is no longer the living body of Christ. It becomes an institution, a thing rather than a living body. It is no longer the presence of the spirit realized, but the presence of the spirit hidden. The institution becomes the prisonhouse for the spirit. Thus in the institution the spirit is not active, because the spirit is imprisoned by the power of externalization. When the spirit is locked into the system of institution, it becomes a storage for the relics of the past and the penitentiary house for the spirit. Unless it releases the spirit to be active, it remains to be the oppressor of the spirit. Those who serve the community which is extremely institutionalized may act as if they are the executioners of their own master, the spiritual presence of the Change. Release the spirit! Let the spirit act according to the very nature of the Change! The highly organized institution is like the tensely built-up muscles which produce nothing but frustration and anger. When the institutional organization is dissolved, the spirit may move freely and direct the people to the creative possibility.

The Church ought to be the community where the spirit is fully manifested. When the spirit is manifest in it, it is open to all people and to all things. Any segregation is an alien element in the Church when the spirit is manifest. The spirit is universal and indiscriminate. Since the spirit is present in all things that exist, the Church becomes the most inclusive community of the spirit. The Church is more inclusive than the community of people. It is cosmic in nature. The beauty of nature shares the manifestation of the spirit. When the presence of the spirit is realized in nature, nature becomes part of the Church. The singing birds and dancing trees are part of that universal congregation. For those who are isolated from nature are in principle segregationists, who cannot be the members of the universal Church. The Church is the community of the spiritual presence in which both the living and the dead, both the animate and the inanimate, belong together in harmony. Thus the Church is more than the congregation of people. It is inclusive of all things. The Church begins with creation and creation is renewed through it. The world is renewed through the renewal of the Church. And this renewal will continue indefinitely.

The Church is a redeeming community of those who follow the process of the Change. It is the community of reconciliation between man and man, between man and nature and between the inner and the external world. The spirit is the power which brings the separation of all things together into a harmonious union. The Church, therefore, is the community of fellowship, the fellowship among all things in the world. Everything is reconciled and nothing is alienated in the Church. In the Church the hostility between man and nature is overcome by the spirit. There is no conflict of nature with man in the Church. Man and nature complement each other. Thus the Church is the pioneer and the focal point of the cosmic harmony.

XV. Family

The family is the primary category of the Church. The family is then the spirit realized in the most intimate group of people and nature. It is a sacred community, because the presence of the spirit is realized in it. The spirit is manifested in the fellowship of husband and wife, as well as parents and children. Because of the spirit in the family, their relationships are complementary to one another. Both the male and the female or husband and wife are in opposite characters, but complementary in their marriage. It is the spirit which is active in their mutual response which makes them one. The story of creation points to the first family on earth. Adam and Eve constitute not only the first family, but the first Church, the archetype of all communal fellowships. Thus the perfect harmony between Adam and Eve before the fall was the ideal family, the primary category of the true Church. The perfect harmony is then the goal of perfect family. The harmony between parents and children is also possible because of the spirit. Without the realization of spiritual presence there is no wholeness of family possible. The relationship between parents and children forms the vertical dimension of the spiritual manifestation in the family. On the other hand, the relationship between the husband and wife forms the horizontal dimension of spiritual realization. The vertical realization of the spirit can provide the continuity of the old, while the horizontal manifestation of the spirit makes the regeneration of the new possible in the family. Thus in both dimensions the spirit can move freely to create the sacred community of family life.

The family of our civilization tends to be the one-sided realization of the spirit. It becomes mainly the horizontal dimension of family life. It is the husband and wife—or the male and female—centered life. The horizontal dimension of life can produce new elements in the family, but it does not give the steady basis for its continuity. It fails to bring about the tie between the old and the new. It stresses tradition less, so that it is easily disintegrated. When the horizontal dimension of life alone is stressed, it can create a lack of the vertical dimension of life in the family. Thus the lack of vertical realization of the spirit creates the increasing rate of divorce. On the other hand, there is another tendency to stress the vertical dimension of life alone. In this kind of life, the relationship between the parents and children becomes the most important in the family. This tendency can make possible continuity of the old but can not produce a sufficient regeneration of the new. Thus the new elements are not easily created in this kind of family life. The ideal family needs the balance of both the vertical and horizontal dimensions of life. The relationship between parents and children must be inseparably related to the relationship between the husband and wife. They are mutually inclusive and inseparable in every affair of family life.

The family does not become a sacred community because of religious conviction. It becomes sacred because of the spirit, the inner power of harmony and unity among the members of family. What makes the family sacred is not something coming from outside, but the inner presence of the Change. As long as the family has its foundation on the inner presence of the Change, it is the community of the sacred. Sacredness is the inward realization of the Change, which alone maintains the harmonious relationship between the vertical and horizontal dimensions of life. In this harmonious relationship the element of sacredness, the power of inner self, is freely manifested in the family life. Whenever the spirit is active in the family, the conflict and disorder is overcome and complementary relationship between the opposites is possible. Thus, in complementarity of the opposites, the harmony of family is retained. This harmony is the expression of the sacred, because it is the way of the Change.

The union of the male and female can be the experience of the most sacred moment in life if the union is in a perfect harmony. That is why sex has been associated with the object of the sacred, even in the beginning of human history. Sexual union properly is based on the fulfillment of the mutual needs. It is to express the total commitment of the self-giving and the self-receiving love. Without this type of commitment the act of sexual union is not proper. The presence of love, the essential quality of union, makes the union of the two persons proper. The self-giving and self-receiving love are perfectly complementary when the union is the expression of the sacred. In the moment of perfect union both man and woman are unconscious of themselves and reach to the bottom of their existence. In this bottom of their existence, they experience the void, the source of all things and matrix of all creation. Thus in the perfect union of male and female the sacred experience of nothingness is possible. However, the union in itself is not sacred but the sacredness is present at the union because of the spirit. Thus marriage is an expression of the sacred and the primary category of the Church, the community of the spirit.

The sacredness of marriage has been recognized by the Church for a long time. The Church, however, is guilty of attempting to make the marriage sacred by the use of sacred rituals. It is not the sacred ritual that makes the marriage sacred. The sacredness is not given from outside of marriage. If the marriage is sacred, it must be within it. The sacredness of marriage is not given by the sacred power of the Church, but is inherent in the very nature of marriage itself. The marriage is a sacred expression because of the spirit, which makes the harmonious union of the opposites possible. The sacredness is realized by the manifestation of the spirit, the power of inner union, that is, the realization of the Change in all relationships. The marriage is a symbolic manifestation of the spirit, which is possible by the very act of union between the opposites. Thus the Church simply recognizes the inherent quality of sacredness in the marriage, for she stands for the sacred.

In a harmonious marriage, male and female ought to be in a complementary relationship. Male is yang and female is yin. Yang is firm, active, creative, self-giving, etc., while yin is tender, yielding, receptive, self-receiving, etc. The virtue of male is then in his firmness, while that of female is her tenderness. The virtue of male is in his active creativity, while that of female in her receptive yielding. The inward quality of male, that is, yang, must be complementary to that of female, yin. The virtue resides not in the difference of character but in the quality of excellence. The excellence of yin is equally significant to that of yang. Thus the ideal wife, for example, is the one who develops the quality of yin, while the ideal husband is the one who develops the quality of yang. The excellence of yin and yang qualities can make an ideal marriage. The roles of wife are the roles of yin and those of husband are those of yang. The tragedy often results in marriage when the confusion of roles between husband and wife arises. Wife is yin and husband is yang in principle, but the reversal often occurs in practice. Wife is below and husband is above, for below is the dimension of yin and above is that of yang. Wife is left and husband is right, for left is the direction of yin and right is that of yang. The confusion of these roles between husband and wife results in trouble. It must be clear that the above is neither superior nor inferior to the below. Right is neither superior nor inferior to left. The active is neither superior nor inferior to the receptive. Neither should wife think that her receptive role is less significant than the active role of her husband, nor should

95

husband feel that his active role is more important than the receptive role of his wife. The virtue is in the excellence of inherent quality.

The roles of parents and children also adhere to the same principle of complementary relationship between yin and yang qualities. Parents represent yang and children yin. Their mutual relationship according to yin and yang qualities makes the family truly concordant. Without peace and harmony in the family there is no peace in the world. The family is the microcosm of the world. Thus the chaos of family life is also the chaos of world civilization.

XVI. Value

It is in the family where one is first taught what is right and what is wrong. He has to *learn* what is good and what is evil. Thus when a child is born, he is expected to conform with the established norm of values. He is not given a chance to develop the original and natural inclination of his own set of values. He is not allowed to respond spontaneously to his intuition of what is good and evil. He has to adhere to the established categories of either good or evil in his ethical decisions. He either has to abide by or to react against the established norms. Thus he is imprisoned within the "either-or" classification of values. He has to think of things in terms of either good or evil, either right or wrong, and so forth, in order to be accepted in the world. According to this category of value judgment, what is not good is always evil and what is not right is always wrong. However, what is good doesn't have to be evil. It can be neither good nor evil. What is right doesn't always have to be wrong. It can also be neither right nor wrong. The either-or way of thinking, the rational category, absolutizes values. There is no possibility of value between these two extreme categories of either-or. The either-or way of categorization is based on the state of being. Values in the either-or way of thinking are not compatible with the world of constant change or transformation.

97

Values in the process of becoming are understood only within the "both-and" way of thinking, that is, the way of faith. What is good is also evil in some aspect, and what is evil is good at times. Good is not a perfection of good and evil is not the totality of evil. They are relative in the categorization of values. Nothing is absolute in the process of becoming. Everything is relative to the Change. Good is not separable from evil and evil from goodness, because they are within the realm of constant change and transformation. Good is not absolutely good, but is relative to evil. It is good because of evil, and evil is realized because of good. Thus when one speaks of good, he also presupposes the existence of evil. When he speaks of evil, he also implies good. When Jesus said to overcome evil with good, he knew that good is inseparable from evil. To overcome evil with good presupposes the inclusion of evil in good. Thus all the values that are valuable are not known in the either-or but in the both-and way of thinking. It is faith that apprehends true value in the changing world.

It is a grave mistake to value the progress of economic productivity, the expansion of political power, the sophistication of tools, the exploitation of nature, high living standards, or hard work. Man's retreat to nature is often regarded as bad, while his conquest of nature is regarded as good. The former is associated with the sign of weakness, while the latter with that of strength. We tend to value the advancement of our civilization and the exploitation of our surroundings. This kind of value judgment is alien to the norm of real value. Jesus never said that the conquest of nature is good. He lived in harmony with nature rather than in conflict with it. He spent much time in nature. He himself retreated to nature for meditation and prayers. He did not want us to arm ourselves with the weapons of technology to conquer nature. Rather, he admired the weak and helpless child as the symbol of goodness. He valued more the natural thing. He devalued the things which came out of man.[1] Jesus did not say that it is good to be am-

---

[1] Mark 7:20.

bitious for self-advancement. He devalued self-centeredness. He valued the man of humble suffering much more than the man of pride and wealth. He who wants to be the first would be the last, and he who wants to be the least is the greatest of all. A criterion for values is not the human achievement; neither is it only the spiritual values. The norm for real values is *naturalness*. As it is said in the story of creation, "God saw everything he had made, and, behold, it is very good."[2] That which makes value valuable is naturalness. What is natural is valuable. Thus it is said, "For from within, out of the heart of man, comes evil thoughts, fornication, theft, murder, adultery, coveting, wickedness, deceit, licentiousness, envy, slander, pride, foolishness. All these evil things come from within, and they defile a man."[3] The intrinsic value which makes things valuable cannot be created by man, but it is inherent in the process of natural becoming. Man cannot create the value but has to find it in his union with the Change, the innermost essence of all becomings. Certainly, the real value lies in the naturalness of an unadorned infant, not in the aggressive personality of the grown adult.

What is natural is always good, and what is unnatural is evil. Naturalness is expressed in the creative process of becoming, while unnaturalness is expressed in the imitative mode of being. Anything that is good has the power of creativity. On the other hand, the power of evil attempts to recreate the created. It is the power of imitation, which comes from the ability to discriminate one from another. That is precisely why the concept of evil is related with the fall of Adam. Through the fall man becomes the likeness of the Creator, the imitator. "Then the Lord God said, 'Behold, the man has become like one of us, knowing good and evil.'"[4] He is different but similar to the Creator, for he is the imitator. His power to imitate the divine creativity enables him to build the glorious civilization of our time,

---

[2] Genesis 1:31.
[3] Mark 7:21-23.
[4] Genesis 3:22.

and becomes the likeness of the Creator, the imitator, because of his sin. Thus sin is the beginning of our civilization and of our unnatural inclinations. What man produces through the power of imitation is then evil, and what is procreated naturally is good. Man shares both what is good and what is evil, because he is both natural and unnatural. In him both good and evil are inseparably intertwined together.

Creativity includes both the regeneration of the new as well as the degeneration of the old. Thus good deals with more than the procreation of the new. It also includes the process of disintegration of the created. It consists of both life and death, for they are the counterpoles in the creative process of the Change. Since growth and decay are the ways of the Change, good is part of the constant change. On the other hand, evil is the product of being rather than of becoming. Anything that has to do with the state of being is evil. Being is an illusion of becoming, for everything is in the process of becoming. Evil is not a reality in the world of becoming but in the world of being. Since the real world is in the process of becoming, evil is essentially unreal, even though it is existentially evident. The state of being is an impossibility in essence, but is experienced in human existence. Thus evil is only an existential one. Evil does not have its roots deep within the inner essence of man. It does not have the last word to say about the destiny of man and the world. It is like the dry leaf on the living tree. It is more than an illusion but less than a reality. Therefore, evil is within good, and good has evil in it. Everything is a manifestation of the Change in a final analysis. Thus, "Everything works for good."[5] It is the Change which will eventually make everything good. The Change works to change all that are existentially unchanging. Overcoming evil with good we may be one with our inner presence of the Change. Since evil is not essentially real, to unite ourselves with our own essence is to become good. Ultimately

5 Romans 8:28.

everything is the manifestation of the inner essence. The cosmos is in the process of becoming toward the full realization of its essence, the inner presence of the Change, which alone transcends the distinction between good and evil or between right and wrong. The process of this realization is known in time.

XVII. Time

Time is a central category of the Change. The Change is known through time. Time reminds us of the changing world. It is compared with the sign-post of the Change. It constantly reminds us that the world is not a state of being, but the process of becoming. Thus time stands for the Change. It is not time which changes the world, but the Change changes time. Time is an expression of the changing process of the world. When time moves from the past to the future, the process of the Change continues from the old to the new. The creative process of the Change from the old to the new through production and reproduction is expressed in the movement of time. Thus time moves in a certain pattern, the pattern of the Change. The Change leads time, and time follows it and expresses its movement. Time is then the servant of the Change. It cannot exist without the Change, while the Change is not known to us without time. Thus both time and the Change are mutually dependent on each other.

Time is commonly divided into three different parts of movement: the past, present, and future. However, in reality it has only two different dimensions: the past and the future. Since time is the process of becoming, the present is not in a state of being. The present is not the being that exists by itself. It is then a boundary line between the past and the future. The present is not a being of now, but the now is becoming in which the past is directed to the future. Now is both the past and the future at the same time. It is neither the past nor the future, but the combination of both at the same time. Thus the present is none other than the continuum of both directions of time. To be in the present is to be in both the past and the future at the same time. In the present both of them become one. Since the past is the category of the old and the future that of the new, the present is both the old and the new at the same time. Thus in the present everything comes together in union. The old is also the new and the new is also the old in the present. To be in the present means to be in the whole time, the time of undifferentiated, that is, the symbol of hope. Thus hope always deals with the present, while wish is devoid of the present.

The present is, then, time undifferentiated. It is neither the past alone nor the future alone, but both of them at the same time. Thus the present is not to be apprehended by the category of the either-or way of thinking. The present is known only in the both-and way of thinking. The either-or way of thinking divides the past from the future and isolates the present from them. Thus the reason which deals with the either-or category of thinking cannot apprehend the present as the undifferentiated continuum of whole time. It attempts to see the present as the state of being rather than as the process of becoming. Faith, on the other hand, sees the present as the whole time, where the past and the future are united together. In faith, that is, in the both-and way of thinking, the reality of time as a whole is understood. The whole time, that is, now, is eternity.

Time always moves from the past to the future. It never moves from the future to the past. This direction of time gives its meaning. Time that has its meaning is history. History is the inclusion of meaning in time. Thus history is time with its meaning. History is then relative to time, for meaning is pregnant in time. The movement of time is also that of history. Time has its meaning in its limitation.

Without its limitation it is no longer meaningful. Time becomes history because of its direction within a limited scope.

The delimitation of time from beginning to ending is based on the process of the Change. However, the beginning is not *essentially* different from the ending of time because of the Change. The beginning marks the creation of the world, and the ending the new creation. The new creation is nothing but the returning to the old creation, the beginning of creation, that is, the creation before the fall. The destruction of the world at the end of time (or *eschaton*) deals with the destruction of the estranged world. Thus the final destruction makes the world return to the original beginning of the world. Certainly, the old world, the world before the fall, is identical with the new world which is to come at the end of time. Thus the end is the beginning again, but this beginning is a new beginning of the old. This new beginning is essentially one with the beginning of the old, but *existentially* different. Therefore, in essence time does not change from the past to the future, for both the beginning and the ending of time are one in the Change. It is said, "The Change is the Alpha and Omega, the beginning and the end." The Change is both the beginning and the ending of time at the same time. Thus this undifferentiated time is the essential time or eternal time, that is, the essential category of the Change.

On the other hand, the differentiated time from the beginning to the ending is an existential time, the temporal time, that is, the existential category of the Change. Both eternal and temporal (or existential) times are inseparable. They move within the limits of endless span, the cycle of the unending journey of change and transformation. History moves in cyclic patterns rather than in linear ones. The goal of salvation history is the end of time, the end of hostile powers, that is also the beginning of the renewed. The end is not the end of heaven and earth, but the beginning of new heaven and new earth. The end of Jerusalem is not really the end, but the beginning of new Jerusalem.

This new Jerusalem is the old Jerusalem renewed at the end. Thus the end is the renewal of the old and the beginning of the renewed. The end is then also the beginning. Thus time moves in the form of a circle, for it is the way of the Change. It is, then, man's illusion to think that time moves in a linear way. The linear time is an illusory time which is based on the state of being.

Just as the dimension of change is different in each manifestation, the time span of cyclic moment, the span between the beginning and the ending, varies according to the varieties of manifestation. Nothing in the world is exactly identical because of the constant process of becoming. Thus nothing has the exactly identical span of time in the world. The time span of a blade of grass is different from that of a tree. The time span of the pine is different from that of the oak. The time span of one pine is different from that of other pines. Nothing has a span of time identical to another. Thus everything has its own time span. Because of the infinite varieties of manifested time, time never itself repeats the same course, even though it moves in the same pattern of birth and death, beginning and ending, or the new and the old. That is why time never repeats itself but renews itself without repeating the identical path. The infinite variety of concrete and manifested time makes the infinite variety of changes possible. Nevertheless, the eternal time, the essential time, that is, the undifferentiated time, is the same yesterday, today, and forever. Thus time is essentially a continuum, but existentially differentiated. The former deals with latent time, and the latter with manifested time. Both latent and manifested times are inseparable. The former is the inward realization of changing process, while the latter is the outward manifestation of changing process. The perfect realization of inward process in the outward manifestation is the goal of history, which is known as the perfect realm of the Change.

XVIII. The Perfect Realm
of the Change

The perfect realm of the Change is more than a mere political symbol; it is the symbol of total salvation. It is the cosmic symbol of renewal and regeneration. It is the perfection of all things, whether the living or the dead or whether the animate or the inanimate. The perfect realm of the Change is the symbol of the grand harmony of all things in the universe. In it nothing is in dichotomy, but all is in complementarity. The Change itself is fully realized in the process of becoming. It is the final and total realization of essence in existence. No one asserts his own inclination to be unnatural when the perfect realm of the Change comes. The process of the Change is no longer interrupted by existence. The very nature of the inner self is fully expressed in the outward self. Everything is in accordance with the principle of the Change. Thus the perfect realm of the Change is the symbol of perfect harmony and union, that is the perfection of love in all things.

The perfect realm of the Change means the perfect manifestation of the Change in all the unchanging phenomena. All the realm of being is to be changed to the realm of becoming in it. The realization of the Change has already been present in the beginning of all things. Its coming is not really coming, because it has already been present. Its

106

coming is its realization by the unchanging. Thus the perfect realm of the Change means uncovering the presence of the Change in the world. It has been buried and hidden in an outward manifestation like the treasure of priceless pearl under the ground.[1] It is in the world like the seed cast on the ground.[2] It is also like the leaven hidden in a bowl of dough. It is not an external manifestation but the inner reality, which has already been in the world without revealing its power. This inner reality has been hidden by the existential estrangement. But it began to be realized by the coming of Jesus as the authentic man, the man of perfect realization of the Change. Thus the coming of the perfect realm of the Change is to be in the process in which the essence of all becomings is realized in existence. When existence is totally realized by essence, the Change will fully reign all things and any attempt to stop the process of becoming will be nullified.

The final and perfect realization of essence in existence, the ground of all becomings, is most of all peace between nature and man. It is a mistake to think that natural expressions and divine will are in conflict. In reality the will of the divine or the way of the Change is not in conflict with nature. Rather it is in conflict with the world of the estranged, which is the unnatural world. Naturalness is the spontaneous expression of the Change. Man in his original nature is not in conflict with nature, for he is a product of nature. Man's hostile attitude to nature comes from his ignorance. By ignorance, nature is seen as an enemy. It is this illusion which has made nature alien to man. Nature has to be exploited in order to demonstrate the divine-like humanity. Thus, out of ignorance an illusion of conflict between man and nature is born. Out of this illusion man has developed scientific technology. By the use of this technology, man finally conquers nature, the mother of his own existence. Nature becomes the raw material for man's hungry stomach. As soon as he has conquered nature, he

---

[1] Matthew 13:44-46.
[2] Matthew 13:3-8.

107

realizes that he has also been conquered. He becomes the victim of his own victory. The war that man fights against nature cannot be won. However, when the perfect realm of the Change is fully realized, the war between nature and man is over and peace will prevail all over the world. It is to be the genuine peace where mutual freedom is granted and the mutual needs are met. Thus the central symbol of the perfect realm of the Change is peace between man and nature. In peace man no longer possesses the aggressive desire to dominate nature. In the perfect realm of the Change, everything lives together in harmony and peace.

The perfect realm of the Change does not come unless nature is restored to its original status, the status before man's exploitation. Without restoring the defeated to the original status the harmonious union between them is not possible. In order to restore it, man must remove that which hinders peace. That is the pollution of nature. Unless the pollution is removed from nature man cannot reconcile himself to nature. The removal of pollution is possible only through purification. This purification makes the salvation of the whole cosmos possible. If the perfect realm of the Change is the most inclusive symbol of salvation, it is also the perfect symbol of purity in all things. To be in peace between the opposites means to be pure in their relationship, which enables them to see their own essence. In purity the transparency of essence to existence is possible. Thus unless the pollution of nature is removed, the conflict between man and nature continues and the perfect realm of the Change does not come. The removal of pollution in man alone does not bring peace in the world.

The perfect realm of the Change is a symbol of new creation. It is the finalization of the future and the end of time. However, the end is also the beginning of the new. New creation is nothing but the returning to the old creation, the creation originally manifested at the beginning. Thus the realization of new creation is nothing but the returning to the undefiled nature, the originally manifested nature before man's exploitation. It is then the new beginning of the original world. The central symbol of this new creation is the new Jerusalem, which is the concentration of the sacred presence, the center of essential becoming to all things. Thus the appearance of the new Jerusalem in the Book of Revelation is the new realization of essence, the coming of the perfect realm of the Change, which is also the original realm of the world. The estranged world has the nostalgia to return to the primordial home of becoming, the matrix of the universe. Thus it is the goal and the aspiration of all things. For this aspiration, history moves according to the process of change and transformation. We are in the stream of this process, the process which is deeply affected by the archaic nostalgia. This inspiration for the original home unites everything in the world toward the ultimate fulfillment of all things in harmony and peace. Then, the perfect realm of the Change may come in our existence as it is in essence.